THE ARCHITECTURE OF
DELANO & ALDRICH

HIGH LAWN

William B. Osgood Field
Lenox, Massachusetts

ABOVE

Entrance facade

RIGHT

Garden baluster with family crest

OPPOSITE

Entrance facade

HIGH LAWN
Lenox, Massachusetts

OPPOSITE

*Garden facade with bas-relief by
Gertrude Vanderbilt Whitney*

ABOVE

Garden facade with pool

LEFT

Playhouse

HIGH LAWN
Lenox, Massachusetts

ABOVE LEFT
Mantel, dining room

ABOVE RIGHT
Main hall

OPPOSITE
Stair

KNICKERBOCKER CLUB

New York City

OPPOSITE

Stair hall

RIGHT

Café

KNICKERBOCKER CLUB
New York City

ABOVE
Reading room

RIGHT
Library

ARTIST'S STUDIO

Gertrude Vanderbilt Whitney
Westbury, New York

ABOVE

Interior

Photo: Karen Radkai. Courtesy of *House & Garden*,
Condé Nast Publications, Inc.

RIGHT

Garden

Photo: Karen Radkai. Courtesy of *House & Garden*,
Condé Nast Publications, Inc.

OHEKA

Otto H. Kahn
Cold Spring Harbor, New York

ABOVE AND RIGHT
South facade and gardens

OHEKA
*Cold Spring
Harbor,
New York*

TOP LEFT
Front entrance

TOP RIGHT
*Bedroom
dormer*

RIGHT
*Swimming
pool*

OPPOSITE
Entrance hall

OAK KNOLL

Bertram G. Work
Mill Neck, New York

ABOVE

Detail, east facade

RIGHT

Entrance facade

OAK KNOLL
Mill Neck, New York

OPPOSITE

Pergola

ABOVE

Still pool, entrance court

OAK KNOLL
Mill Neck, New York

ABOVE

Stair hall

OPPOSITE

Dining room

WALTERS ART GALLERY

Baltimore, Maryland

ABOVE
Loggia

RIGHT
Stair detail

OPPOSITE

Entrance stair leading to central court

GEORGE F. BAKER, JR. HOUSES

New York City

GEORGE F. BAKER, JR. HOUSES
New York City

LEFT
Dining room
Photo: © John M. Hall

BELOW
Main hall
Photo: © John M. Hall

RIGHT
Living room
Photo: © John M. Hall

UNION CLUB

New York City

LEFT

Locker room

ABOVE

Original card room

UNION CLUB
New York City

CLOCKWISE FROM TOP LEFT

*Backgammon vent, original
backgammon room*

Peacock vent, west room

Sconce, original backgammon room

*Mantel and light fixture, original
card room*

THE ARCHITECTURE OF
DELANO & ALDRICH

PETER PENNOYER AND ANNE WALKER

FOREWORD BY ROBERT A. M. STERN

NEW PHOTOGRAPHS BY JONATHAN WALLEN

W. W. Norton & Company
New York • London

HALF-TITLE

Top left: Frieze, Oak Knoll
Top right: Knickerbocker Club
Bottom left: Frieze, 1040 Park Avenue
Bottom right: Niche, drawing room, High Lawn

For information about permission to reproduce selections from
this book, write to Permissions, W. W. Norton & Company, Inc.,
500 Fifth Avenue, New York, NY 10110

Composition and book design by Abigail Sturges
Manufacturing by Friesens
Production Manager: Leeann Graham

Library of Congress Cataloging-in-Publication Data

Pennoyer, Peter.
The architecture of Delano & Aldrich / Peter Pennoyer
and Anne Walker; foreword by Robert A.M. Stern.
p. cm.
Includes bibliographical references and index.
ISBN 0-393-73087-5
      1. Delano & Aldrich – Criticism and interpretation. 2.
Delano, Williams Adams,   1874-1960 – Criticism and
interpretation. 3. Aldrich, Chester Holmes, 1871-1940 – Criticism
and interpretation. 4. Architecture – United States – 20th century.
I. Walker, Anne. II. Title.

NA737.D45 P46 2003
720'.92'2—dc21

                                                        2002038657

W. W. Norton & Company, Inc., 500 Fifth Avenue,
New York, N.Y. 10110
www.wwnorton.com
W. W. Norton & Company Ltd., Castle House,
75/76 Wells St., London W1T 3QT

0987654321

CONTENTS

FOREWORD

With this book we come one step closer toward recovering the lost history of twentieth-century architecture. By this I do not mean to refer only to the work of twentieth-century Traditionalists, of whom William Adams Delano and to a lesser extent his partner Chester H. Aldrich were among the most accomplished, but also to the work of so many Modernists as well, like Wallace Harrison, Morris Lapidus, or Edward Durrell Stone, who, because they did not conform to the narrow and rigidly bounded definition of the so-called International style were derided by critics and until recently also ignored by historians. Now, a new generation of scholars is helping us, step by step as it were, to see the recent past whole. They do not sit in judgment but, instead, straightforwardly present the work, and the circumstances that made that work possible, for us to consider, evaluate, and enjoy. So this is a book for Traditionalists and Modernists alike. Indeed it is for all who love architecture as the art of building beautifully.

Much of the history of Modernism has been suppressed by generations of polemically blinkered historians who have for too long allowed themselves to be bounded by the stylistic arguments of the 1920s and 1930s. As a result, the fate of the history of Traditional architecture has been even more parlous – trapped as it has been in, among other things, political theorizing, pseudopsychology, and a nostalgia for the good old days. As a consequence, our understanding of the trajectory of Traditional architecture's place in twentieth-century culture is muddled. Moreover, the sheer lack of published documentation has been shocking, so that the work itself has become fugitive. While innumerable books present and represent every last detail of the works of pivotal Modernists like Le Corbusier or Frank Lloyd Wright, and of other significant figures like Richard Neutra, the work of very few Traditionalist architects is well documented. True, there is a three-volume memorial on Lutyens's work, but even that is not an *oeuvre-complet* such as we have for Le Corbusier. Similarly, knowledge of Charles Platt's work is largely confined to the early part of his career, well known through the reprint of a 1913 monograph, but there is no comparable presentation dealing with his work from that time to his death in 1931.

Things are now changing, with some excellent monographs by young scholars. Keith Morgan's book on Platt does give us the big picture, if not enough pictures or drawings of the work. Elizabeth Dowling's book on Philip Shutze is superb in almost every way, with beautiful illustrations, but Karen Hudson's study of her father Paul Williams, though lovingly conceived, in neither scholarly enough nor detailed enough. While the focus has been on country-house architects possibly a reflection of the fact that there is a market for such books among the affluent general public, little attention has been given to those firms that did so much to shape our public environment. Robert Bruegmann's study of the Chicago firm specializing in office buildings Holabird & Roche is the kind of book every first-rate firm deserves, a meticulously researched and intelligently reasoned text accompanied by excellent and profuse illustrations. Still, Carrère & Hastings, architects of libraries, clubs, and country houses, and Warren & Wetmore, who did much much more than New York's Grand Central Terminal, have yet to be documented in a proper publication of any kind, while the recent book on the protean John Russell Pope, though scholarly, is both under-illustrated and somewhat apologetic for the work itself.

Walker and Pennoyer's *Delano & Aldrich* does not attempt to be exhaustive, but it is thorough and scholarly, combining solid research with careful formal description and analysis to constitute a significant building block to be added to the reconstruction of our architectural history. Its even-handed presentation is a model of tact, enabling us to appreciate the work and the social and professional milieu that made it possible. If it is a bit impatient with the firm's late "modernizing" work, it is never dismissive or judgmental. The authors have let Delano speak for himself, quoting liberally from his unpublished autobiography. Best of all they have let the work speak for itself in period photography and drawings to which are added superb contemporary photos by Jonathan Wallen, John Hall, and Karen Radkai that taken as a whole cannot help but make the enduring beauty of the work obvious to a new generation of students, practicing architects, and the general public, many of whom are entrusted with the responsibility to preserve and maintain this incomparable legacy of architecture.

I greet this book with complete enthusiasm. It comes none too soon, just as many of Delano & Aldrich buildings, critically neglected for so long, without a scholarly apparatus to support them, are threatened with demolition or thoughtless "renovation." This book gives great pleasure and renewed energy to carry on the important work of preserving the legacy of our twentieth-century masters, Modernist and Traditionalist alike.

—*Robert A. M. Stern*

THE ARCHITECTURE OF
DELANO & ALDRICH

INTRODUCTION

On the evening of October 29, 1928, Delano & Aldrich celebrated its twenty-fifth anniversary of practice in the main hall of New York's Architectural League. The firm, established by William Adams Delano (1874–1960) and Chester Holmes Aldrich (1871–1940) on drafting tables borrowed from their mentor, Thomas Hastings, had grown to be one of the most productive and accomplished architectural practices of the first half of the twentieth century in America. The turnout for the event was tremendous. The hall was festooned with hundreds of silver balloons and "great garlands and bunches of grapes hanging on the walls in perfect Owen Jones."[1] Six hundred of the firm's clients and friends spent the evening enjoying good company, food, and music, and saluting the two architects.

The occasion held significance for the firm as well as for American architecture. The party, it was claimed in *Time*, answered the question "Who builds them and makes them beautiful?" of the houses springing up on fashionable Long Island and the many clubs and schools that were adding character to the streets on the Upper East Side of Manhattan.[2] While they clearly profited from fortunate timing, Delano & Aldrich's commanding position in their profession sprang from their ability to couple an astute understanding of the ruling class with an architecture distilled from traditional sources. Their fluency and talent were well directed and produced a refreshing body of work that was personal, modern, and distinctly American.[3]

By 1915, Delano & Aldrich had supplanted McKim, Mead & White as the premier architects of New York City clubhouses and, in 1927, had just been chosen for the new Union Club, an enviable commission and a rare grand project to survive the Depression. As the last great building the firm was to complete in Manhattan, the Union Club (1932) was also one of its most distinct. A superb modern classical design, it was executed with a spirit and lightheartedness that only Delano & Aldrich could achieve. The Depression dramatically altered the world in which the architects were working, but as commissions for clubs and mansions dwindled, the firm continued to forge ahead, making its mark in a series of important government projects.

Delano & Aldrich, along with such contemporaries as John Russell Pope, Harrie T. Lindeberg, Charles Platt, David Adler, and Mott Schmidt, were working during a period when American architects had authoritative command of the classical vocabulary. The full-bodied voluptuous architecture of the fin-de-siècle had celebrated America's coming of age as a world power with a view that abundance was the highest goal in architectural language. In response to the heavy, cluttered taste of the so-called "brown decades," the new generation of architects, of which Delano & Aldrich were leaders, shaped and developed American taste, producing a style leavened with erudite abstraction and sparing composition.[4]

As Delano & Aldrich's architecture evolved, it became increasingly distilled, yet the partners continued to set their own pace. Aware that their work was a holdout against the rushing tide of Modernism, they were not iconoclastic in their approach, adopting a stripped-down classical style appropriate to their public commissions completed in the 1930s and 1940s, just as they had adopted Georgian and Neoclassical styles that suited their domestic projects of the 1910s and 1920s. While they designed buildings that were thoroughly modern in terms of program and function, ranging from expansive country estates to airports, Delano & Aldrich were never moved by the idea of an aesthetic based on the expression in form of a building's function. Ever true to their Beaux-Arts training, they shaped each project around a legible and functional plan, regardless of its density, size, or program. Without feeling any insecurity in its increasingly isolated position, the firm remained staunchly opposed both to architecture as a "machine for living" and to the modernistic tendency to discard the spiritual qualities of the art.[5] As Delano wrote, "I am a strong believer in tradition but tradition tempered with motion."[6]

Delano was emphatic in his belief that "Architecture [was] an Art."[7] As their style evolved, the architects never wavered in their convictions or strayed from the fundamentals—"the innate quality of proportion or heritage in the past"—in their quest for enduring beauty.[8] Through their work, Delano & Aldrich demonstrated the programmatic adaptability and the expressive versatility of traditional ideas and forms. The architecture of Delano & Aldrich stands as an enduring statement of the American genius for interpreting classical precedent and achieving modern expression.

BACKGROUND
AND BEGINNINGS

William Adams Delano was born in the parsonage of the Madison Square Presbyterian Church in New York City, where his grandfather, Dr. William Adams, was minister. The Delano family was only distantly related to the Franklin Delano Roosevelts; Delano's father, Eugene Delano, was also of Huguenot descent; his mother, Susan Magoun Adams was a direct descendant of the John Adams dynasty; and his first cousins were Browns, of the venerable merchant bank Brown Brothers & Company.[9] William A. Delano was brought up in a world where vacations in Europe, summer retreats, and the Ivy League were simply the charted course of a gentleman's coming of age.

The young William A. Delano was fun-loving, curious, and impressionable. In 1880, Eugene Delano joined the staff of the Brown Brothers' Philadelphia office and moved the family from New York to 1705 Locust Street. He later commissioned Theophilus P. Chandler to design a summer house in Bryn Mawr. Watching this "very good-looking, well-dressed man, who rode over on a well-turned-out horse" supervise the builders, William A. Delano at once chose his future profession. "In short, I was hypnotized by him and the whole performance, and then and there decided to be an architect."[10]

The Delano family also summered in Orange, New Jersey, where Delano's Adams grandparents had a large Victorian country house set high on the brow of Orange Mountain overlooking the Newark Plains and New York City. Here, Delano spent many charmed summers among his four siblings and six Brown cousins as well as neighbors such as General George B. McClellan.[11] In 1885, after both Adams grandparents died, the family sold the summer retreat, but the Delanos and the Browns continued to summer together, migrating to the more rustic reaches of Pasque Island, one of the Elizabeth Islands off the southeast shore of Massachusetts.

After early schooling by governesses, Delano was sent to The Lawrenceville School in New Jersey, from which he graduated in 1891. He went on to Yale University, where he soon stood out among his classmates; not only did he have no interest in participating in sports, but also he was the only one of his set to elect courses in drawing and painting.[12] He joined sophomore, junior, and senior societies, made many friends (some of whom would become clients), and enjoyed the social aspects of college to their fullest. It was during this time that Delano's father transferred to the New York office of Brown Brothers & Company and settled the family at 12 Washington Square North, a Greek Revival townhouse that, along with the twelve adjoining houses east of Fifth Avenue, formed an impressive row on the northern edge of the park. Delano was to recall fifty years later that "this house had a great influence on my architectural thinking."[13] "The simple rooms, with their large windows and high ceilings, taught me that these elements [were] more important than elaborate decorations, which people tire of in time."[14] The essence of the house—the simple but well-proportioned brick facades, the tall double-hung windows, and the *piano nobile*—were to appear often in Delano's work throughout his career.

After graduating from Yale, which offered no formal training in architecture, Delano went directly into the architecture program at Columbia University, established in 1881. At Columbia, Delano studied for two years under Professor William R. Ware, who gave the "most delightful talks on art, morals, literature— anything that interested him at the moment." Delano studied drawing and the orders under Maximilian K. Kress and William T. Partridge, mathematics under Frank Dempster Sherman, and rendering under Charles Alonzo Harriman. In his course on the history of architecture, he found that A. D. F. Hamlin had a "great knowledge of his subject," but he "presented it without inspiring his pupils to inquire further into the spiritual and economic causes."[15] As part of the School of Mines, Columbia's architecture curriculum stressed the practical rather than the artistic; the teaching was dry and uninspiring.[16] "On a whole, those first two years at Columbia offered little to an enthusiastic approach to architecture. Bill Emerson, long Dean of Architecture at M.I.T., and I had drawing boards side by side. We took our work very seriously, both being Puritans at heart and having

12 WASHINGTON SQUARE NORTH
New York City, c. 1940

Municipal Archives, Department of Records
and Information Services, City of New York

blown off steam at our respective universities, but to us Columbia in those days was like going back to Kindergarten."[17]

Heartily discouraged, Delano was further shaken in his choice of career when he won a poster competition for Colgate Perfumes "in which many well known painters took part." To find out whether his talents did lie in the realm of architecture, Delano left Columbia and entered the office of Carrère & Hastings in 1898 to "learn what architecture really was."[18] John Mervin Carrère and Thomas Hastings had formed their partnership in 1885 after training at the Beaux-Arts and in the offices of McKim, Mead & White. By 1898, their practice had grown into one of the leading Beaux-Arts firms in New York. It was here that Delano befriended Chester Holmes Aldrich, a graduate of Columbia in the midst of his studies at the Ecole des Beaux-Arts, as the two young men worked together— Delano in a minor capacity—on the firm's competition entry for the New York Public Library.[19] Delano was captivated by office life, and his commitment to architecture was cemented when the firm's design was selected.

After a year at Carrère & Hastings, "imbued with the Beaux-Arts spirit," Delano was drawn to Paris, the natural progression for a budding architect exposed to the talents of Hastings and his colleagues. Before his departure, Delano and Aldrich agreed to form a partnership when Delano returned.[20] In Paris, Delano spent four months studying for the entrance examinations to the Ecole under Georges Gromort in Victor Laloux's preparatory atelier, and was tutored in mathematics by Harvey Wiley Corbett, already a student. In 1899, Delano was the first foreign applicant admitted to the school. Though his performance in the architecture, drawing, and modeling portions of the examinations was strong, his outstanding score in mathematics put him near the top of the entering class.[21]

The atelier was the nucleus of the Beaux-Arts system. While students were given lectures and instruction at the Ecole, they studied design in a studio under one architect, or *patron*. A camaraderie formed between students in an atelier as they competed monthly with the other studios on *projets* that were judged by the Ecole. Delano studied under Victor Laloux whose atelier, established in 1890, was favored among American students; alumni of Laloux's studio also included such notable American architects as William Lawrence Bottomley, Arthur Brown, Jr., George Chappell, John W. Cross, William Emerson, Harold P. Erskine, Henry Shepley, Lawrence Grant White, and William Van Alen. Laloux's principles were to shape Delano & Aldrich's approach to architecture. As Delano recalled, "he impressed upon the pupils in his atelier the importance of a simple, coordinated and easily read plan, from which would rise a well composed mass."[22] Delano received his diploma from the Ecole in 1902 after a successful academic turn, and after his grand tour he returned to join Aldrich in 1903.[23]

Chester Holmes Aldrich's childhood was not quite as urbane as Delano's. He was a native of Rhode Island who, according to Delano, had "a good deal of New England in [his] character."[24] He was born on June 4, 1871, into the prominent Aldrich family of Providence, to parents Elisha and Anna Aldrich. Elisha Aldrich's father had owned a dry-goods business, and Anna Gladding Aldrich was the granddaughter of a Providence ship captain. While the Aldriches lived modestly, they were civic minded and intellectually cultivated; Chester and his three siblings grew up in an artistic environment that included the Providence Art Club and such family friends as Sidney R. Burleigh, a prominent Rhode Island artist. Their upbringing encouraged ambition and self-improvement. Chester and his siblings Richard and Amey left Rhode Island to attend Columbia, Harvard, and Smith, respectively, most likely on scholarships; Chester and Richard were to rise to the tops of their professions, Richard as a renowned music critic for *The New York Times*. Amey was an avid (although unpublished) writer, and brother John, an engineer and watercolorist, became president of the New England Butt Company in Rhode Island. Chester spent his early years in Providence on Congdon Street and summered with his family at Sakonnet Point, an unspoiled corner in Little Compton, Rhode Island.[25]

Perhaps at the urging of Sidney Burleigh, Aldrich left Rhode Island to attend Columbia University, from which he received his first architectural degree in 1893. After traveling abroad for two years sketching and studying the great monuments of antiquity, he entered the Ecole des Beaux-Arts in 1895, having passed his entrance examinations with flying colors—the first out of about two hundred applicants. Aldrich enjoyed a successful run at the Ecole, winning several medals in the second class alone. He joined the Daumet-Girault-Esquié atelier and studied under Pierre Esquié who had won the Grand Prix de Rome in 1882. While the Esquié atelier was not as large as that of Laloux's or as popular among American students, it was as successful at capturing the sought-after Grand Prix.[26]

In 1898, Aldrich took a leave of absence from the Ecole to return to the United States in order to be near his parents, who were both gravely ill. Aldrich's rendering skills were well known among Beaux-Arts draftsmen and during this period, he worked in the office of Carrère & Hastings, where his artistic talent as a watercolorist helped the firm win the competition for the New York Public Library. Aldrich returned to Paris and received his diploma from the Ecole in 1900. He then rejoined Carrère & Hastings for the three-year period during which his future partner was still abroad. When Delano returned in 1903, the two architects joined forces, continuing to work out of their mentors' offices while they looked for their own space.

The years spent in Europe were enlightening for both emerging architects. Delano, who had been a mediocre student at Lawrenceville and Yale, hit his stride at the Ecole. Described by classmate Louis E. Jallade as "indefatigable," he worked hard and flourished in the competitive environment of the Beaux-Arts atelier system.[27] The culture and climate of Paris had a deep resonance for Delano, and he returned often to its architecture for inspiration. Similarly, Aldrich's travels in Italy sparked a lifelong passion for that country and its people. He returned to Italy as head of the Red Cross refugee relief effort from 1917 to 1919 and again to head the American Academy in Rome from 1935 until his death in 1940.

Delano was a handsome man, recognizable, in President Theodore Roosevelt's words, by his "little mustache and genial smile."[28] In 1907, he married Louisa Millicent Windeatt Potter, daughter of Edward Tuckerman Potter, one of the Victorian era's most renowned architects, and the niece of Bishop Henry C. Potter.[29] Described by many as strong willed and strident, Mrs. Delano was also one of her husband's greatest and most valued critics, and despite her harsh disposition the couple could be loving and affectionate. They had one son, William Richard Potter Delano, and one grandson, William

Adams Delano, to whom the architect wrote a compelling 150-page letter recording the story of his life.[30]

Aldrich never married. He and his sister, Amey, were exceedingly close, shared many of the same interests, and lived together their entire adult lives.[31]

The focal point of Delano and Aldrich's New York was the Murray Hill district. The architects lived two blocks apart—Delano at 131 East 36th Street and Aldrich at 116 East 38th Street—and always within walking distance of their office. In the firm's beginning years, they rented space on the third floor of a private house at 9 East 41st Street, and subsequently, above Keppel & Company's print shop at 4 East 39th Street. In 1916, they moved into a stable and milk depot at 126 East 38th Street that Delano had converted into elegant offices. An intimate three-story building, the studio was refaced in stucco and embellished with three French doors and a delicate wrought-iron balcony on the second floor, with round bull's eyes on the third. Reception rooms, a paneled library with antique Dutch paintings, and a small garden were located on the first floor. The partners' offices were on the second floor, and the top floor was a large drafting room lit by three north-facing skylights.[32] While redesigning the building, Delano discovered that its commercial use was in violation of the zoning code in Murray Hill, so he determined to convince the power behind the neighborhood, J. P. Morgan, to grant a variance. The young Delano could be persuasive and, after a personal audience, Morgan acquiesced.[33]

The small studio housed the prolific practice whose designs and alterations, by the early 1950s, numbered over five hundred. According to Delano, office records showed that more than three hundred employees passed through the office during its fifty-year history. However, as productive as the firm was, Delano and

Aldrich did not consider their office to be large, nor did they intend it to be. The principals were responsible for the design and supervision of the commissions they individually won, and in a small office they could be involved personally with each project. While Delano and Aldrich shared commentary and criticism, projects were for the most part attributable to one of the two architects, since each commission was assigned to the partner who brought it into the practice.[34]

With their offices on the second floor, Delano and Aldrich were slightly removed from the activity of the drafting room. Firm associates such as Henry S. Waterbury, James Stewardson, Herbert Godwin, and George A. Licht were directly involved in the development of the designs. The utmost attention was afforded to each project, and often, the firm presented alternate schematic versions of the design to clients. According to one Delano & Aldrich alumnus, George Licht had a strong presence, looming over the drafting room and enforcing the strict standards of the office. A summons to his cubicle would strike terror into a draftsman's heart.[35] Chester B. Price, the renowned architectural delineator, was also closely associated with the firm. In 1924, *Portrait of Ten Country Houses by Delano & Aldrich*, the only monograph on the practice, was published. It featured illustrations by Price and an introduction by the prominent critic, Royal Cortissoz.

Delano and Aldrich fostered friendships, advanced their practice, and influenced their profession through professional, civic, and social organizations. They were members of the Architectural League of New York, the National Institute of Arts and Letters, and the Beaux-Arts Society as well as Academicians of the National Academy of Design and Fellows of the American Institute of Architects. Delano served as president of the A.I.A.'s New York chapter (1928–30) as well as chairman of the Art Commission of the City of New York and trustee of the New York Public Library. They also enjoyed club life: both architects were members of the Century Association, the Coffee House, and the Digressionists, and Delano belonged to the Knickerbocker Club, The Brook, and India House.[36] For eight years between 1903 and 1911, Delano also found time to teach at Columbia, where the architecture program was in the process of being reorganized along the lines of the Beaux-Arts atelier system.[37]

Socially, both men had the advantages of an easy and engaging manner and the polish of a European education. Such culture and erudition were valued assets to Americans who were becoming more committed to the arts in study and in practice. Delano was determined to make a mark for himself and for his clients. Although soft-spoken, he could also be forceful. As an early client observed: "McKim was stubborn but you're more so."[38] He was assertive without being either aggressive or intrusive. "He did not push [his opinions] but let them speak for themselves; and he spoke always . . . in very gentle tones, always offering his views tentatively; such as 'How is this?'"[39]

Delano's facility for friendship was remarkable. He was a faithful correspondent and a loyal friend; his collection of letters at Yale vividly illustrates how he touched scores of his contemporaries with his charm, charisma, and devotion to the field of architecture. Aldrich, too, in Delano's words, had a "genius for friendship."[40] He was "invariably just, helpful, gay and refreshing in companionship. For he was endowed with many genuine and satisfying amiabilities." His friends

OPPOSITE

DELANO & ALDRICH OFFICE
126 East 38th Street, New York City
Delano & Aldrich Collection, #63852,
Collection of the New-York Historical Society

"enjoyed those qualities, and came to listen for his ready laughter and soft, clipped speech."[41] In a eulogy to the architect, Royal Cortissoz described Aldrich as having been "busy in diverse directions, in architecture, in the Academy, in music, in philanthropy, in social life. . . . He was a man of his time and had his share of sophistication. But it was to the high admonition of his inner self that he gave heed. If, wherever he went, he diffused an atmosphere of goodness, it was because he kept himself unspotted from the world."[42]

While Delano was almost exclusively absorbed by his architectural career, Aldrich had many outside interests, particularly watercoloring, music, and religious history. He spent considerable time actively participating on the boards of directors of his favorite organizations—the Greenwich Settlement House, the Italy-America Society, and the American Red Cross. He was especially devoted to the Kips Bay Boys Club of which he served as president for twenty years, and the Aldrich Farm, his country retreat on Staten Island for convalescent boys from city hospitals.[43] Since his activities often took him away from the office, he did not win as many commissions as his partner. Of its huge catalogue of commissions, the firm recorded just thirty-three projects as "The Principal Works of Chester Holmes Aldrich."[44]

From all accounts, Aldrich was the quieter and more retiring partner. Delano recollected that "perhaps if [Aldrich] had been a more original dynamic person our partnership would not have endured for 35 years for I am afraid I was too often headstrong in carrying out my ideas."[45] While at the height of their productivity in 1924, when Delano was single-minded in his devotion to architecture, Aldrich would take time to write a long article for *The New York Times Sunday Magazine* on "the 700th anniversary of the day on which St. Francis received the stigmata on a wild and lonely mountaintop at La Verna, Italy."[46]

Delano leaned on Aldrich and appreciated his steady nature. Aldrich's stable personality strongly complemented Delano's more volatile and hard-working character. Aldrich, in turn, admired his partner's intensity: "In all the years that I've worked with him, admiration has just kept on growing. I've never seen his enthusiasm flag, I've never seen his ideas grow stale, I've never seen his taste waver, and chief of all, I've never seen him slacken in that thing which we're always told is the very essence of genius—the 'infinite capacity for taking pains.'"[47] The partners enjoyed their tenure together and, even after Aldrich's departure in 1935, Delano never changed the firm's name.

The partners had the good fortune to start their practice in New York during what has been called the "age of metropolitanism."[48] Following the surging expansion of the economy as industrialization took hold, New York became the nation's capital of arts and business. Delano and Aldrich were perfectly positioned where these two worlds overlapped. The rapid economic growth spawned unprecedented wealth and produced a great number of rich men with a taste for art and culture. With their family and school connections, the young architects were well prepared to enter society's upper echelons.

As urban and financial centers flourished, the popularity of country life grew proportionately. In the late nineteenth century, New York was still a city of private houses but the wealthy were relocating uptown to palatial residences in newer, more fashionable neighborhoods near or along Fifth Avenue. At the same time, this moneyed group continued to seek out retreats in the country, establishing themselves in vast baronial mansions, known as "cottages," in fashionable areas outside the city. Since the 1870s, social New Yorkers had been making the pilgrimage to summer colonies like Newport, Rhode Island, Lenox, Massachusetts, and Bar Harbor, Maine. In the 1880s and 1890s, enormous estates maintained by dozens of servants—such as Peabody & Stearns's Elm Court (1886–1900) for William Douglas Sloane in Lenox and Richard Morris Hunt's The Breakers (1892–1895) for Cornelius Vanderbilt II in Newport—became the preferred mode of leisure living among the country's leading families.

Following the turn of the twentieth century, city dwellers turned to landscapes within the new range of the access provided by automobiles to establish second homes. Americans grew increasingly inclined toward sports and leisure as a balance to the grind of the city, and as a result, country clubs—the social hub of country life—with golf courses, tennis courts, polo fields, and hunting grounds, proliferated.[49] Within the circles in which Delano and Aldrich moved, there were scores of potential clients with the desire and the wherewithal to build country houses within driving distance of New York. The architects found themselves at the center of this movement as they forged a name for themselves as one of the country's preeminent house designers.

The rise of country house development was essentially a suburban phenomenon. Generally, estates were composed of the main house, which was scaled for family, guests, and entertaining; estate buildings, which included garages, barns, sheds, and stables; formal gardens, often associated with certain public rooms of the house; and the kitchen court, drying yard, and cutting gardens, which were frequently obscured from the more visible portions of the landscape. Despite their extensive gardens and numerous outbuildings, estates were typically situated on smaller plots of land, an effect that gave rise to a number of spacious suburban enclaves in Long Island, Westchester, and New Jersey. While barns and stables made up a portion of the property—in the tradition of the English gentleman landowner—they were often only used recreationally. A look at any issue of the American edition of *Country Life* from this era shows how much the ideal country retreat emulated the great estates of the landed gentry of England: between the advertisements for Lincoln sedans and Tiffany jewels were sections featuring pedigreed hunting dogs, prize roosters, and hens.[50]

Among the upper classes of society, trends in architectural styles spread quickly. As early as 1877, McKim, Mead, and White had traveled throughout New England studying its early architecture and seeking new design inspiration; they rediscovered the Colonial idiom and its English variant, the Georgian, and reinvented them as American styles. In the 1880s, this reinvention took shape with the seemingly sprawling shingle style or modern colonial house with "shrewdly placed bays and towers, saner decoration, intelligently studied skyline and more urbane interiors."[51] The shingle style, which flourished in resort areas in the 1880s, gave way to Beaux-Arts extravagance in the 1890s. Newport's Bellevue Avenue was rapidly transformed into a showcase of immense palazzos and chateaux culminating in Cornelius Vanderbilt II's colossal family home, The Breakers, on Ochre Point. As the shingle style fell out of favor, McKim, Mead & White responded to the

JOHN D. ROCKEFELLER ESTATE
*Kykuit, Pocantico Hills, New York,
c. 1909*

building frenzy, designing its share of ostentatious mansions modeled on European sources. By the 1900s, the firm had returned to simpler American models in creating its designs.

The success of their designs for H. A. C. Taylor (1884–86) in Newport, a center hall house with Palladian windows and classical details, and for James L. Breese (1898–1900) in Southampton, a southern Colonial Revival design with a monumental porch, illustrated the emerging, quieter, classical taste. Their Georgian designs for city houses, such as that for H. A. C. Taylor at 2-4 East 72nd Street (1894–96), James J. Goodwin at 9-11 West 54th Street (1896–98), and Charles Dana Gibson at 127 East 73rd Street (1902–3), also proved to be popular stylistic alternatives to the more prevalent and elaborate French styles. As influential and visible New York figures such as Andrew Carnegie and Senator Elihu Root commissioned houses in the more reserved styles, the movement toward a simplified and inherently more dignified architecture gained momentum.[52] McKim, Mead & White also adopted the red brick Georgian prototype as a model for clubhouse design, executing clubs such as the Harvard (1894), Lambs' (1904–6), and Colony (1905–6) that displayed a simplified interpretation of classicism more American in spirit than their Italian-influenced counterparts: the Century Association (1889–91), Metropolitan (1891–94), and University clubs (1896–1900).

Delano and Aldrich emerged onto the architectural scene at a moment when it was possible to definitively influence American taste. The first Americans to be trained at the Beaux-Arts—Richard Morris Hunt, Thomas Hastings, H. H. Richardson, and Charles McKim—had given the profession a standing within society. Delano and Aldrich found themselves entering a field where talent was in demand and commissions abundant. Each of the architects acquired one of the firm's most prestigious clients within their first year of practice: Henry Walters and John D. Rockefeller, Sr. Delano met Walters, a wealthy Baltimore business-man and art collector, on his grand tour as Delano visited with his college friend Cornelius (Neilly) Vanderbilt III aboard Vanderbilt's yacht, *The North Star*. Walters enjoyed Delano's company on buying forays in Venice and, in a leap of faith, invited the young, inexperienced architect to design a museum for his extensive collection in 1904. The Walters Art Gallery (see pages 76–79) was an amalgam of two architectural precedents, one French and one Italian: a hôtel in Paris designed by Félix Duban and the Palazzo Balbi in Genoa, built during the seventeenth century.[53] The exterior details, interior loggia, and vaults were exquis-itely executed. However, the building so clearly followed its European prototypes that it did not seem to be, as Delano described his later work, "stamped with my personal feeling."[54] Though it was an impressive and ambitious early project, the young architects were unable to synthesize their inspirational sources into a cohe-sive, personalized composition.

Kykuit, the Rockefeller home in Pocantico Hills, New York, could have been one of the firm's most important and prestigious house commissions. It was, however, so fraught with client interference and involved so many designers that the project became a thoroughly compromised effort.[55] The Rockefellers' previous house on the property burned in 1902. While new designs were pre-pared by the father's favored architect, Dunham A. Wheeler, John D. Rockefeller, Jr., asked Chester Aldrich (a distant cousin of his wife's), then work-ing at Carrère & Hastings, to prepare a competing design to upset his father's choice. The designs rendered by Aldrich eventually won out; however, John D. Rockefeller, Sr., insisted that elements of Wheeler's plans be incorporated into the house. Further stripping the young firm's authority, W. Wells Bosworth was put in charge of the landscape and outbuildings, and, to the irritation of Delano and Aldrich, the talented and older Ogden Codman joined the project to design the interior architecture.

Completed in 1908, the finished house was as unpalatable to the Rockefellers as it was to the architects and was quickly redesigned by W. Wells Bosworth with Charles Platt acting in a supervisory role; Delano and Aldrich were orphans in the new team. Although their experience at Kykuit was bitter, the architects showed a brilliant grasp of the principals of Beaux-Arts planning in relating the house to the dramatic topography of the hilltop site overlooking the Hudson. That their attempts at an integrated American style were not at first successful was as much due to the imposition of their clients as it was to inexperience. As the firm found its stride, the wooden qualities of its early commissions were transformed into elegance.

WALTERS ART GALLERY
Baltimore, Maryland, 1904–09

Delano & Aldrich Collection,
Avery Architectural and Fine Arts Library,
Columbia University in the City of New York

STYLE AND ARCHITECTURE

The architects were interested in creating human-scaled architecture that reflected their personal interpretation of precedent while accommodating their clients' needs. *For You to Decide*, Delano & Aldrich's self-published handbook, was the first step in that realization. The small booklet, which led the client through the particulars of construction, was created to satisfy the client's list of "fixed ideas on various details."[56] With these details decided, the architects were then able to advance the design "from an artistic point of view." An amusing tract, *For You to Decide* was both informative on such "important matters" as the architect's claim on the interior architecture and landscaping and dismissive on such mundane details as closet finishes—"We believe that it is an exploded theory that the smell of cedar keeps out moths." Some sections seem to be a transparent attempt to thwart client inquiries on the subject: "Some people want a burglar alarm system installed, others prefer the burglar" and "a garbage incinerator in the kitchen . . . is not recommended where there is a pig." Other parts such as a comparison of double-hung windows and casement windows offered trenchant advice that is still relevant.

In the booklet, the architects advised that "the design of the gardens and terraces surrounding the country house [were] essential parts of the architect's work."[57] This conviction extended to their city practice; the architects were always aware of context and used site limitations to their advantage. Delano, the more prolific designer of the two partners, generally "avoided thinking of the new job until [he had] seen the site and examined it carefully," for "a glimpse of a vista here or a tree there or even the roll of the ground might give you the inspiration you are always hoping for."[58] The architect carried a small pad in his pocket and sketched out solutions as they came to him; the sketches were then drawn to scale at the office.

In keeping with the Beaux-Arts method, a functional and legible plan underpinned each Delano & Aldrich project. Since the architects considered landscape an extension of the house, external features often informed room arrangement; sunlight, prevailing breezes, and topography were considered essential in the siting of a house. Though some of his most striking country house designs were built on inclines, Delano generally avoided hilltops unless there was a substantial plateau on which to build. He tried to "put the entrance door on the north side, and by the same token the staircase, for [those] elements do not require sunlight as the living room and bedrooms do."[59] Typically, primary rooms were organized *en filade* and tied to features within the landscape by strong axes. As a result of their meticulous planning, the firm's buildings were always well sited with amply lit interiors and views.

Charles Platt has been credited with inspiring Delano & Aldrich's generation of architects to establish a close relationship between landscape design and architecture; however, this group had more immediate influences. Although Platt was the first American to publish a record of Italian gardens, a book found in many important architectural offices, the architects who studied in Paris at the turn of the century had direct experiences of the formal aspects of European garden and landscape design to inspire them. Though Delano and Aldrich held overriding control in the design of landscapes around their projects, they worked alongside such landscape architects as Beatrix Farrand, Umberto Innocenti (Innocenti & Webel), Olmsted Bros., Ferruccio Vitale (Vitale & Geiffert), and Annette Hoyt Flanders.

The architects' grasp of history also provided them with the vast resources to shape the architectural expression of their work. Reflecting on his years at the Beaux-Arts and his grand tour, Delano wrote that "I . . . so absorbed all the architectural books and the buildings themselves that they were a part of me. When I came into practice I rarely opened a book except to refresh some memory."[60] In most Delano & Aldrich designs, traditional models served as the basis for interpretation but did not present hard and fast examples to copy. Inspired by historical examples, Delano & Aldrich created more personal and abstracted renditions that reveled in the power of classical proportion and pure form. Elements from sources as varied as the houses of Washington Square and the Colonial South or Palladian villas were distilled to such a degree that they became almost abstract in the process. For example, the round arch

JAMES A. BURDEN ESTATE
Woodside, Syosset, New York, c. 1924

Delano & Aldrich's simple, open brick arcade supports the side passage connecting the west wing to the central portion of the house.

Mattie Edwards Hewitt. Nassau County Museum Collection, Long Island Studies Institute

PAUL MELLON ESTATE
Brick House at Oak Spring,
Upperville, Virginia, 1946

Gottscho-Schleisner, Inc. Prints and Photographs
Division, #303622, Library of Congress

was a recurring motif in each Delano & Aldrich project, within and without. However, with no imposts, they departed from an iconic reading of classical form; their beauty lay in their pure shape and essential proportions. Although it is possible to identify examples of Delano & Aldrich's work modeled on specific landmarks—such as Paul Mellon's Brick House at Oak Spring, Upperville, Virgina, based on William Buckland's Hammond-Harwood house in Annapolis, Maryland—in many commissions sources were buried deeper.[61]

Delano and Aldrich also approached interior architecture with the same sense of assurance as they did their exteriors, viewing their design as simply another extension of the architect's realm. The partners felt strongly that the architect—one architect—"must be in control" of the house and its interiors "if the design is to be a success" and brought a similar rigor and plasticity into their rooms.[62] Harmonious proportions and crisp abstraction contributed to an effect of elegance and calm. The architects designed all of the hardware in their interiors, including pelmets and stair rails. Curtain pockets that insured that the draperies would not obscure casings and paneling, and sweeping spiral stairs were also distinctive features. Delano and Aldrich insisted that they be the authors of a room's interior finishes—"the fixed or built-in portions of the room, such as paneling, plaster ornaments, and electric light fixtures;" however, their booklet, *For You to Decide*, also made clear their sensitivity to issues that affect the decorator's part—"the furniture, rugs and hangings."[63]

VICTOR MORAWETZ ESTATE
*Three Ponds, Woodbury, New York,
1930*

*Sun parlor with murals by Victor
White. The firm often created rooms
where the architecture was set inten-
tionally as a background to murals.*

Mattie Edwards Hewitt. Nassau County Museum
Collection, Long Island Studies Institute

Delano and Aldrich always saw artistic collaboration as the highest goal for its
rooms and were supportive of the decorator, the artist, and the artisan. In many of
its buildings, the firm created major rooms where the architecture was set inten-
tionally as a background to mural art.[64] The firm also worked closely with artists—
such as Robert Winthrop Chanler and Howard Gardiner Cushing—as well as
woodworkers, stone carvers, and ironmongers to complete its schemes. The architects considered elegant light fixtures essential to their rooms and delighted in their
design. In early projects, such as the Knickerbocker Club, they were simple and
more classical in inspiration whereas in later projects, such as the Union Club, they
became more exuberantly Art Deco.[65]

Delano was unapologetic about the firm's grounding in tradition: "There is as
much that is new to be said in architecture today by a man of imagination who
employs traditional motives, as there is in literature by an author, who, to express
his thought, still employs the English language."[66] Sound traditions and familiar
forms made sense to the architects, as they did to their clients, whereas Modern
architecture, without "reference to the nature and dignity of man" did not.[67] The
partners considered their work modern in spite of its historical undertones. They

used new methods of construction and advanced technology, producing designs that reflected the spirit of the modern age. According to Aldrich, if they "handled the design with freedom and answered the needs of our present day clients, it [would] really be expressive of our own time . . . The result of whatever we do shows in itself . . . the seal of our own hand."[68]

Delano & Aldrich can be grouped with a number of competing architects—such as Harrie T. Lindeberg, David Adler, and John Russell Pope—who were also looking to diverse historical sources to shape a modern idiom. In *The Architect and the American Country House 1890–1940*, Mark Alan Hewitt discusses the forces that shaped this rise of "domestic eclecticism" at the turn of the twentieth century. A cast of select architects, for the most part academically trained, and the era's "tastemakers"—business and society leaders—fed off of each other's interests propelling the movement forward. The architect who sought to forge a new expression based on history and the discerning client with distinct ideas about comfort and established cultural traditions perpetuated eclectic architecture until World War II.

The partners understood the delicate balance that existed between patron and architect and strove to satisfy their clients without lowering their own standards. Most of the firm's commissions came through Delano and Aldrich's considerable

ABOVE

CUSHING HOUSE

121 East 70th Street, New York City

First-floor hall with murals by Howard Gardiner Cushing

A. B. Bogart. Delano & Aldrich Collection, Avery Architectural and Fine Arts Library, Columbia University in the City of New York

BELOW

KNICKERBOCKER CLUB
Lighting fixtures

Courtesy of the Knickerbocker Club, New York City

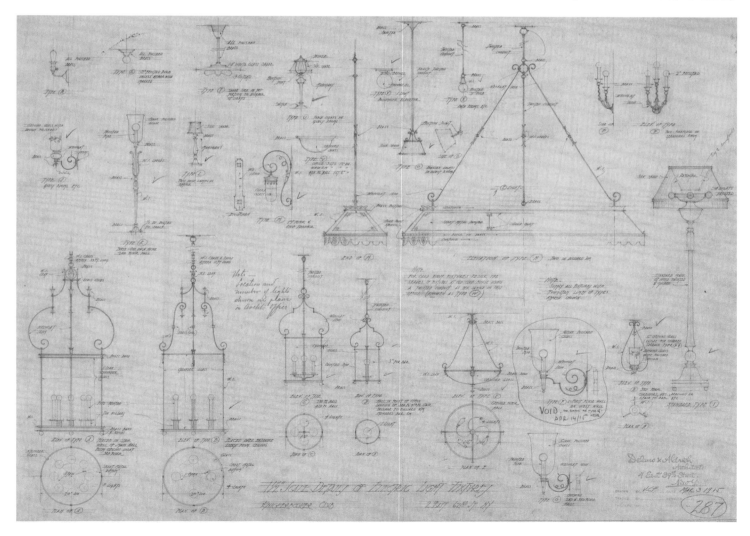

connections. Delano in particular considered each building or house a story about its owners, and often incorporated clever details and symbols into their design that would tell something of its occupants.[69]

The architects were impatient at the inclination of the public to apply stylistic labels to their projects. Delano found it "such a deadening thing to have to follow a particular style slavishly. To do so is copying and nothing more. Yet most people want to call their houses Georgian or Norman or Palladian, and are not satisfied with accepting a good house, well arranged, without a fancy name."[70] While Delano & Aldrich's approach to architecture was scholarly, it differed from the more archeologically correct work of McKim, Mead & White. Like the architecture of their mentor firm Carrère & Hastings, Delano & Aldrich's work was increasingly spare and interpretive. The partners considered their work novel—a new twist on tradition—and gauged their competitors accordingly. Delano wished John Russell Pope, the "gifted artist" with whom he served on the Board of Architectural Consultants in Washington, D. C., "had not been such a close follower of precedent for he had the ability to express himself more personally without losing the spirit of what he sought."[71] In comparison to Paul Cret with whom Delano identified more closely, "Pope scrupulously followed the Classic; Cret digested it and gave it a new expression."[72]

With its economy of decoration and freeness of spirit, the quality of a Delano & Aldrich design lay strictly in the essentials. Compared to some of their contemporaries, their work could almost be described as "nonstylistic." Their simple brick and stucco cottage, a model the architects used repeatedly, defied historical typecasting and was singled out by historian Talbot Faulkner Hamlin as manifesting the "trend toward free, nonstylistic design, as opposed to historical or even eclectic design."[73]

The firm's reliance on a rational plan, proportion, and taut form often instilled palpably picturesque qualities, however unintended. The architects did

MISS E. R. HOOKER HOUSE
New Haven, Connecticut

The firm's understanding of proportion and material allowed them to create interpretative, free designs.

Kenneth Clark. Hamlin, *The Pageant of America*

ROBERT S. BREWSTER ESTATE
Avalon, Mount Kisco, New York

*Treillage transforms the west porch
into a picturesque garden pavilion.*

Delano & Aldrich Collection,
Avery Architectural and Fine Arts Library,
Columbia University in the City of New York

not set out to create picturesque compositions and believed "the picturesque [was] something which happen[ed] of itself. It [was] not something to start out for or to manufacture." The tendency toward the "willfully picturesque," they held, led "to all sorts of vagaries, to restlessness, and above all, to a neglect of essential architectural values."[74] In their efforts to avoid an indefensible mode of design, they seemed to have hit upon an architecture that could be attractive while striving toward more abstract and profound ambitions. It was precisely this ambition, perhaps learned in the rarefied atmosphere of the Parisian atelier, that set them apart from their competitors.

Their thoughtful abstraction made Delano and Aldrich the authors of a modern and American paradigm. With their personal twist on tradition and their reliance on the fundamentals of space and form, they were able to move past style per se, in the creation of architecture especially suited to their own era. By simply remaining true to the essentials, Delano & Aldrich was able to move easily between building types, some unprecedented, and transition into the period after the Depression. In the process, they built a substantial body of work with incredible range and ingenuity.

COUNTRY HOUSES

Delano & Aldrich was closely involved in the creation of one of the country's most fashionable enclaves at Muttontown on Long Island, about fifty minutes by train from New York.[75] In 1903, prominent New York attorney Bronson Winthrop purchased 450 acres in Muttontown and Delano & Aldrich built its first important country house for the Winthrop family known as the Egerton L. Winthrop, Jr., house or Muttontown Meadows (1903–4).[76] In the design of the Winthrop house, Delano, the principal architect of the estate, fused two architectural influences into one composition as he had at the Walters Art Gallery. While the exterior of the house clearly referred to Mount Vernon, its interiors were delicately scaled and French in inspiration. The house, with facades of white painted wood milled to imitate stone, was set on a rectangular brick terrace and tied to the landscape through strong axes centered on an orchard, fountains, and formal gardens beyond. The paneled drawing room, the small morning room on the main axis to the garden, and the graceful library showed that Delano was capable of a delicately scaled and elegant interior architecture that imbued the house with an almost feminine character.

The Muttontown enclave grew as Muttontown Meadows was joined by Delano's cottage, Muttontown Corners (1910–11), a larger estate for Bronson Winthrop, and a house for diplomat Lloyd Griscom (c. 1920) who married a Winthrop cousin, as well as Muttontown Lodge (1926) for Delano's friend Paul Hammond. Delano built his own informal summer retreat, Muttontown Corners, on ten acres of Bronson Winthrop's property. Situated on a sloping site with apple trees, the house was a simple, comfortable, stucco cottage with a gabled roof and window openings dressed in brick.[77] The multiple gables and sweeping rooflines gave the house a picturesque quality despite its spare facades. While the gardens, designed in collaboration with Beatrix Farrand, were not as formal as they were on the firm's larger estates, they had a subtle relationship with the house that underpinned their gradual, unfolding sequence. At Muttontown Corners, according to Royal Cortissoz, "every incident in the garden present[ed] itself in the same just and unassertive fashion."[78] A winding path, opposite the front door, led up the hill to reveal a hidden, bowl-shaped garden where Delano and his friends played boule.[79]

Though Bronson Winthrop's U-shaped house was much larger than Delano's cottage, a similar warmth of spirit permeated the design. It was also detailed with

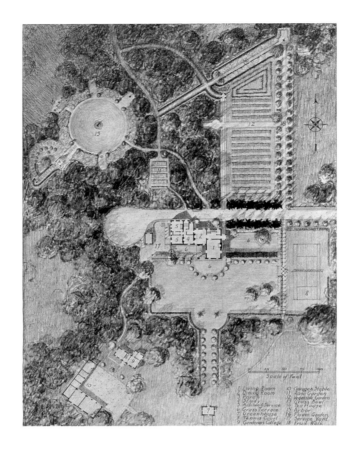

ABOVE

WILLIAM ADAMS DELANO ESTATE
Muttontown Corners
Muttontown, New York

Country Life in America 34 [May 1918]: 68. Courtesy
of the Society for the Preservation of Long Island
Antiquity, Cold Spring Harbor, New York

ABOVE RIGHT

Muttontown Corners

Site plan by Chester B. Price

Cortissoz, *Portraits of Ten Country Houses*

white stucco walls textured with sand, brick trim, and a shingled roof; porches and trelliswork eased the formal symmetry of the building.[80] A formal garden centered off the living room led into a long court defined on three sides by a double row of clipped maples. Another axis extended from the tea house to the north, through the living room, and out to the garden, fountain, and terraces beyond. The swimming pool, breaking from the orthogonal axes of the house, added variety to the plan. Throughout the 1910s and 1920s, Delano & Aldrich used the simple, "non-stylistic" cottage as a model for larger estates. The firm executed a number of spare, stucco houses and buildings with high gabled roofs and brickwork details for Long Island clients such as George Whitney in Westbury (c. 1915), Vincent Astor at Cloverley Manor in Sand's Point (1922) as well as for Mrs. James Wortham at Normandie in Newport, Rhode Island (1914) and Miss Elizabeth Hooker in New Haven, Connecticut (1914).[81]

At the same time that Delano and Aldrich were working in Muttontown, they were also establishing their country house practice outside the reaches of Long Island. The firm's first major essay in the Georgian style was High Lawn (1908–10) (see pages 80–85), the residence of Mr. and Mrs. William B. Osgood Field in Lenox, Massachusetts.[82] Mrs. Field (née Lila Vanderbilt Sloane) had grown up summering at nearby Elm Court, her parents' enormous Lenox cottage; she moved to High Lawn upon her marriage to W. B. Osgood Field. As an early project, the design manifested overt Beaux-Arts influences. The house's brick facades were dressed with emphatic limestone details including quoins, a belt course, and a full-scale cornice supporting a steeply hipped slate roof with dormers, and the ground floor was set with French doors, surmounted by bas-relief panels by Gertrude Vanderbilt Whitney depicting the labors of the farm. High Lawn was also one of

BRONSON WINTHROP ESTATE
Site plan by Chester B. Price

Cortissoz, *Portraits of Ten Country Houses*

WINTHROP ESTATE
Entrance facade

Edward R. Senn. Howe, *American Country Houses of To-day*. Courtesy of the Society for the Preservation of Long Island Antiquity, Cold Spring Harbor, New York

WILLIAM B. OSGOOD FIELD ESTATE
High Lawn, Lenox, Massachusetts

Entrance facade

Delano & Aldrich Collection, Avery Architectural and Fine Arts Library, Columbia University in the City of New York

ROBERT S. BREWSTER ESTATE
Avalon, Mount Kisco, New York

Terrace facade

Delano & Aldrich Collection,
Avery Architectural and Fine Arts Library,
Columbia University in the City of New York

the firm's few houses where a full, freestanding order was employed with massive Doric columns supporting the roof of the bowed terrace leading to the eastern lawn and the monumentality of the main hall expressed with a double Doric colonnade. The architects organized the grounds around strong axes and screened the ultimate view of the Berkshire Mountains from the front, intensifying the experience of this prospect from the east terrace.

Simultaneously, the firm was designing Avalon for Robert S. Brewster, Delano's college friend, and his family in Mount Kisco, New York (1910) (see pages 86–93) in the vocabulary of an eighteenth-century French manor house.[83] While the particulars of the architectural style—the plain stucco walls; the tall, pitched, slate roofs; and the applied treillage—seemed typical of any important house in the neighborhood of Versailles, Delano brought an astonishing plasticity to its expression. Set on a sloping site, Avalon showed Delano's ability to transform a difficult landscape into the basis for an ingenious architectural solution. The entrance court and core of the house were set on different levels. A wing, which doubled as a porte cochere, extended out from the primary rooms to meet the arrival court. This arrangement allowed Delano to relate each of the important rooms to one of the principal features of the landscape: the library and its porch to a path and folly, the Temple of Love; the dining room to a path marked by a fountain; and the arcaded entrance gallery to a rose garden.

In the mid-1910s, the firm executed a series of archetypal commissions, including Gertrude Vanderbilt Whitney's studio and the Burden estate in which they distilled traditional sources dramatically, giving their work a more abstract quality. Delano's studio for artist Gertrude Vanderbilt Whitney (1913–15) (see pages 94–99), Neilly Vanderbilt's sister, was situated on the Whitney estate in Westbury, Long Island. In the studio's bold, Palladian-inspired design, Delano relied on form and geometry to create a powerful and evocative set-piece.[84] The white stucco facade, with its iconic classical balance, was punctuated by a recessed, arched entrance vestibule and two colossal windows with a highly concentrated frieze at the attic level. The crisp lines of the building were heightened in juxtaposition to the charged quality of the frieze. In plan, the building was simple and functional. A small paneled hall, flanked by reception rooms, led directly into the main working space, a double-height room spanning the width of the building, top lit by a massive skylight undisguised by decorative treatment. Exotic murals by Howard Gardiner Cushing, Robert Winthrop Chanler, and Maxfield Parrish were integrated into the interiors, making this commission one of Delano's most complete artistic collaborations.

As a refuge from the Whitney compound, the landscape surrounding the building turned inward, creating a sanctuary and an artistic haven. From the studio, tall French doors opened onto a terrace, its pergola festooned with thick vines of wisteria, where steps led four feet down to the garden. The combination of this depression in the elevation of the garden and the surrounding fencing made the whole space seem as private as a room. A rectangular swimming pool with a pebble border and dark walls blended with the natural palette and resembled a reflecting pool while a narrow rill connected the pool to a round tank at the back of the garden where another semicircular, wisteria-covered pergola complemented the arch of the studio's facade.

In the spirit of a modern country estate, Woodside, the Burden house in Syosset, Long Island (1916–18) (see pages 114–21), was designed for family living and lavish entertaining.[85] The one-hundred acre estate, built for iron and steel industrialist James A. Burden and his wife, the former Florence Adele Sloane—Lila Vanderbilt Sloane's sister—included accompanying garages (1916), stables (1917), a gatehouse (1926), and other service buildings. Inspired by Whitehall, a 1760 house in Annapolis, Maryland, the brick-and-limestone composition of Woodside's center block and flanking wings presented a commanding symmetry and balance. The taut facades emphasized the subtleties of the closely laid Flemish bond. Brick quoins softened the sharp corners of the house, and a soldier course on the facade was used to delineate a shift in floor level. By raising the main floor one level, Delano was able to elevate the public rooms to create a *piano nobile* and raise the flanking galleries, lit by bull's-eye windows, on an arcaded basement that has been compared to Robert Adam's Adelphi Terrace.[86] Again, details were minimal and executed in shallow relief. Only a carved marble keystone marked the entrance to the house, a simple, punched, arched opening with sidelights and a transom in a delicate leaded pattern.

Inside, Delano carefully constructed a sequence of rooms in which each stage evoked a different feeling. A small circular entrance hall enveloped visitors before leading them into the grand oblong stair hall with rounded ends and, directly across, a gallery with a south view of the great lawn. All of the entertaining rooms overlooked the expansive grass terrace while the service areas fronted the arrival court. The grounds, which also included a formal garden twice the size of the house, circuitous paths, and a tennis court, were carefully arranged in an unfolding sequence. The formal garden was placed to the east of the house, visible only after one had stepped out onto the great lawn. Smaller winding paths leading to the tennis court and the serpentine wall alongside the formal garden were revealed in progression as one moved through the landscape. In 1920, the Architectural League of New York awarded the project its Gold Medal of Honor, the organization's highest honor for a building, but the Burden estate was more in the public

GERTRUDE VANDERBILT WHITNEY STUDIO
Westbury, New York

Entrance facade

John Wallace Gillies. Delano & Aldrich Collection, Avery Architectural and Fine Arts Library, Columbia University in the City of New York

JAMES A. BURDEN ESTATE
Woodside, Syosset, New York
Entrance facade, c. 1924

Mattie Edwards Hewitt. Nassau County Museum Collection. Long Island Studies Institute

eye when Edward, Duke of Windsor stayed there when he visited the North Shore in the summer of 1924.

During this period, the firm was also at work on a house in Cold Spring Harbor, Long Island, for Otto H. Kahn, one of the banking world's wealthiest and most powerful men. His estate, Oheka (1914–17) (see pages 108–13), consisted of a 72-room French chateau–style mansion, gardens, bridle paths, outbuildings, stables, tennis courts, and an eighteen-hole golf course.[87] To this day, Oheka is the largest house in America save Richard Morris Hunt's Biltmore (1889–95) in Asheville, North Carolina, designed for George Washington Vanderbilt. It was also home to one of the most extensive French gardens in the country.

Oheka was perhaps the greatest anomaly in the firm's body of work. Delano was palpably embarrassed by the excess of the commission and believed that the house grew "in size as [Kahn's] self-importance grew."[88] In its design, Delano tried to downplay the size of the mansion by expressing the second story windows as dormers with false canopies rendered in lead and by animating the massive roof with patterned roof slates. Despite the magnitude of the commission, Delano exercised restraint, relying more on form and proportion and less on ornament. This quality, coupled with the subtle juxtaposition of material—stucco and stone—brought life to the facades' crisp lines and expansive dimensions. While the shape and design evoked a chateau in the Loire Valley, the abstraction of architectural elements was unprecedented for such a grand estate. Neither classical orders nor elaborate carvings were used to convey its importance.

Bertram G. Work's estate, Oak Knoll (1916–18) (see pages 126–31), in Mill Neck, New York, captured the essence of Delano's tastes more accurately than the Kahn commission.[89] Work was the president of Goodrich Rubber Company. His house, a pure stucco pavilion punctuated by a classical portico, tall windows, and two bull's eyes, was even less ornamented than the Whitney studio. Nonetheless, Delano's subtle wit was visible. Cornices were carved with shells and fish, and Samuel Yellin's intricate ironwork, wrought in scrolling shapes of shells, dolphins, and turtles, was set off against the house's stark facades. The estate plan exhibited the same adept handling of the landscape as seen at Avalon and Oheka. Delano exploited the complicated hillside site to create a complex section of terraces

ABOVE

BENJAMIN MOORE ESTATE
Chelsea, Muttontown, New York

Entrance facade, 1933

Samuel H. Gottscho. Prints and Photographs
Division, #303622, Library of Congress

RIGHT

Chelsea

Garden facade and moat, 1933

Samuel H. Gottscho. Prints and Photographs
Division, #303622, Library of Congress

around the house. Suppressing the service wing one level below, he ensured the presence of the house as a pure form.

The pace of country house production continued to mount through the 1920s. Chelsea, Delano's house for paint manufacturer Benjamin Moore and his wife, Alexandra Emery Moore, in Muttontown, New York (1923–24), displayed the architect's ability to control and distill stylistic influences.[90] The estate, named after the family farm in Manhattan—now known as the neighborhood, Chelsea—was built in stages, the square gallery added in 1929. The Moores saddled the architect with an unlikely basket of inspirations from their travels. Having admired the stark white-and-black-trimmed manor houses on the banks of the Upper Yangtze River and the farmhouses of Provence, they asked Delano to incorporate aspects of each into the design of Chelsea which Delano did, creating a picturesque, white-stucco, U-shaped house with black trim, a steep slate roof, bull's-eye windows, and corner *tourelles* surrounded by a moat on two sides. An arcade, expressed in pure arched form, overlooked the garden court. Landscaping by Umberto Innocenti and Ferrucio Vitale included exotic topiaries, lotus-filled

ponds, a moon gate, and a serpentine brick wall. Interiors included a reception room with a 120-foot mural by José Maria Sert, painted for the house in 1926 and executed in oil paint and white gold. In spite of the client's unusual requests, Delano carried off the design with a resolute hand. According to the architect, the house was among his most admired Long Island projects.[91]

Compared to Chelsea, Little Ipswich in Syosset for Mr. and Mrs. Chalmers Wood (1927–28) was more contained.[92] Mrs. Wood (Ruby Ross Wood) was a pioneer in the field of decorating, having begun her career ghostwriting Elsie de Wolfe's books on the subject. In a rare use of an iconic classical order, Delano delivered a small, stylish, flat-roofed house anchored by a domed temple with a three-bay Doric portico. In articulation, the house was more restrained than the Whitney studio and as simple and pure as a house by Minard LaFever, Greek Revival architect and author of several influential pattern books. The white-painted brick facades with an abstracted cornice and a paneled parapet pierced with a fret motif were graceful and powerful. A characteristically gracious arch led into Delano's interior designed to set off Mrs. Wood's decorative whimsy. The domed entrance hall, painted in faux relief, was more suggestive of a hall in the Palace of Isabella d'Este at Mantua than the interior of a Greek Revival house.

The design of Harrison Williams's tennis-court and swimming-pool building at Oak Point in Bayville, Long Island (1927–28), reiterated Delano's faith in the power of pure form.[93] In 1926, Williams, director of the American Gas and Electric Company, and his wife, Mona, one of the era's most renowned socialites, moved into Dunstable, designed by Babb, Cook & Willard. The couple renamed the estate Oak Point and asked Delano to renovate the vast 80-room mansion and to design a sports pavilion. The tennis-court building's taut brick veneer followed its steel frame, forming a sleek, modern arch. As at Little Ipswich, Delano dramatically enhanced the building's presence by an identifiable classical motif—in this case, a semicircular Ionic portico.

In the 1920s, the firm executed a series of variations on the example set by the Burden house. These commissions included Mirador (1921) (see pages 140–43) in Greenwood, Virginia, for Mr. and Mrs. Ronald Tree; Peterloon (1928–30) (see pages 156–57) for real estate developer John J. Emery in Indian Hill, Ohio; and an extensive estate on the battlefield of Waterloo in Argenteuil, Belgium (1929–30) for William Hallam Tuck, an international businessman with Virginian roots who had married a Belgian heiress. Mirador, built in the 1830s, was purchased by Colonel Chiswell Dabney Langhorne in the 1890s as a summer retreat for his wife and eight children—Irene (who became the model for Charles Dana Gibson's Gibson Girl and subsequently, the artist's wife) and Nancy (who married Waldorf Astor and became the first female Member of Parliament) among them. The estate descended through the family to Langhorne's granddaughter Nancy, then married to Ronald Field Tree, heir to the Marshall Field fortune, who asked Delano to renovate and update it. While Delano's commission for Mirador was ostensibly an alteration, he transformed the rather squat plantation house of the 1830s into a grandly appointed house with his fluid touch.[94] He reapportioned the interior spaces to create a central top-lit rotunda and a curved open stair and extended the rear of the house out over an elegantly attenuated arcaded base. He drew the Blue Ridge Mountains into the backyard by framing the dramatic view with a wisteria-draped pergola, which defined the outer edge of the garden court. Mirador was Nancy Tree's first decorating project; she later became a famous decorator during her marriage to Colonel C. G. Lancaster.

Commissioned on the brink of the Depression, the Emery and Tuck houses were among Delano's last mansion-scaled houses.[95] While they were poles apart in

TOP

MR. AND MRS. RONALD F. TREE
ESTATE
Mirador, Greenwood, Virginia

Garden facade with arcade

Frances Benjamin Johnston.
Delano & Aldrich Collection,
Avery Architectural and Fine Arts Library,
Columbia University in the City of New York

ABOVE

JOHN J. EMERY ESTATE
Peterloon, Indian Hill, Ohio

Entrance facade

Courtesy of the Peterloon Foundation

RIGHT

WILLIAM HALLAM TUCK ESTATE
Waterloo, Belgium

Delano & Aldrich Collection,
Avery Architectural and Fine Arts Library,
Columbia University in the City of New York)

GENERAL AND MRS. EDWIN M.
WATSON ESTATE
Kenwood, Charlottesville, Virginia

Garden facade

Delano & Aldrich Collection,
Avery Architectural and Fine Arts Library,
Columbia University in the City of New York

terms of location, each displayed Delano's distinctive restraint and poise. Like the Knickerbocker Club and the Burden house, detailed brickwork was accentuated in the absence of ornamentation. Delano continued to personalize his own set of architectural elements, including broken pediments with inset ships or shells and carved snail volutes. In tribute to the Emerys' love for animals, he even incorporated a carved basket of puppies into the design of Peterloon. Details were carried out in typically shallow relief; lintels and quoins were emphasized simply by contrasting materials.

After 1930, when the depth of the economic implosion had stripped the architecture profession of much of its optimism and opportunities, house commissions were few and far between. In the 1930s and 1940s, the firm was designing entire houses smaller than the service wings of its earlier commissions. Though budgets hardly allowed the collaborations with artists, stone carvers, and ironmongers that had made the firm's houses so special, clients still looked to Delano & Aldrich for the fundamental structure of a classical house. At Kenwood in Charlottesville, Virginia (1939–41), designed for Franklin D. Roosevelt's Military Aide, General Edwin M. Watson, and his wife, Delano executed an abstract gabled cottage set within the rolling hills below Monticello.[96] In the absence of detail, gracious lines and proportions propelled the austere design forward.

A comparison between Kenwood and Muttontown Meadows, one of firm's first commissions actually inspired by Virginian architecture, illustrates the extent to which Delano & Aldrich's work grew and developed. Muttontown Meadows manifests its French and American inspirations quite literally; the firm had yet to fully interpret and integrate its sources coherently. Kenwood, completed almost forty years later, clearly exhibits the profoundly abstract nature of Delano's mature work. Yet, with such a concise palette, Delano still exerted his ability to design a well-proportioned, distinct house in the continuity of the classical tradition.

NEW YORK BUILDINGS

As Delano and Aldrich began their partnership, New York was undergoing rapid transformation. The city was experiencing the twilight of the era of the private house as cooperative and rental apartment buildings (descendants of the tenement and apartment hotel) began to eclipse the house in popularity, practicality, and economy. Simultaneously, the smaller commercial buildings of the 1890s were giving way to the skyscraper as steel-frame construction and the elevator ushered in the era of the high-rise. Architects such as Cass Gilbert and Ernest Flagg in the 1900s and Ralph Walker and Raymond Hood in the 1920s and 1930s were rapidly reshaping the city's commercial and financial districts with their architecturally distinct skyscrapers and setback towers.

By 1903, Fifth Avenue from the 50s to the 90s was fully developed as the city's grandest residential street. The blocks overlooking Central Park were a tableau of robust mansions and elaborate limestone chateaus. In comparison, the architectural character of Park Avenue was not yet fixed. Until 1904, the trains running beneath the avenue were powered by steam; the fumes billowing out from the railroad tunnels prevented the wide, attractively landscaped boulevard from obtaining status as a desirable settlement for the rich and discerning. When Senator Root, a visible and influential New Yorker, began construction of his house at 71st Street, Park Avenue consisted mainly of tenements and ordinary houses. The electrification of the trains in 1904, however, eliminated the smoke along the thoroughfare and opened the avenue's grounds for redevelopment. Park Avenue quickly grew in popularity, and in 1909 the *Real Estate Record and* Guide noted that "on Park Avenue at the present moment may be seen under construction, simultaneously, both cooperative and individual houses of the highest type in their respective classes," acknowledging the thoroughfare as the "second Fifth Avenue."[97]

While Delano & Aldrich contributed only two buildings to the Fifth Avenue streetscape, the firm played an integral role in transforming Park Avenue and the area surrounding it, designing many houses, clubhouses, schools, churches, and apartment buildings. Despite the rise of the apartment building, there was no apparent decline in the popularity of private dwellings in the area above 60th Street between Fifth and Park Avenues.[98] Delano & Aldrich designed only two apartment buildings, but continued to build single residences and renovate brownstones until the early 1930s.[99]

ROBERT S. BREWSTER HOUSE
*100 East 70th Street, New York City,
c. 1940*

Municipal Archives, Department of Records
and Information Services, City of New York

KNICKERBOCKER CLUB
2 East 62nd Street, New York City

Museum of the City of New York,
The Wurts Collection, #801555

CLUBS, HOUSES, AND SCHOOLS

Early houses for lawyer Allen Wardwell (a Yale classmate of Delano's) at 127 East 80th Street (1912) and artist Howard Gardiner Cushing at 121 East 70th Street (1910) manifested Delano & Aldrich's proclivity for severe, planar facades and minimal decoration.[100] Another college classmate, Robert S. Brewster, commissioned the firm's first large-scale New York residence at 100 East 70th Street, completed in 1908, before the firm designed his country house in Mount Kisco.[101] With its restrained limestone facades, rusticated base, and palazzo-style composition, the design exhibited strong Italian influences. Yet the bold, central cartouche, French windows, and rounded dormers recalled elements of Parisian architecture. Here, Delano attempted to build "a simple and dignified home" "in no particular historic style or epoch" but did not achieve the fluidity of his more mature work.[102]

Delano's commission for the Knickerbocker Club (1913–15) (see pages 100–3), a venerable power in New York's club society, was an impressive charge for the young firm. The clubhouse, on the corner of 62nd Street and Fifth Avenue, was a quiet, residentially scaled building inspired by the houses of Washington Square.[103] The design was notably spare; however, the front entrance, embellished with substantial architectural rhetoric and executed in surprisingly shallow relief, obtained a sculptural quality against the club's planar brick walls. The portico, with almost Baroque exuberance, rose through the marble base to the middle of the facade, signaling the complex, open, two-story arrangement of the entrance and stair hall. Delano raised the first floor a half story above street level, creating a proper *piano nobile*. In designing the club, Delano was able to convince the building committee of the wisdom of pulling part of the building's mass back from the property line on

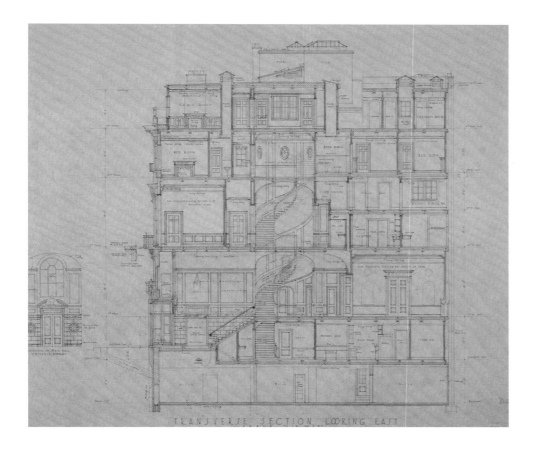

the south side to create a terrace facing Fifth Avenue. While important for light and views, this massing also allowed the clubhouse to be viewed as a freestanding structure from Fifth Avenue, giving it a prominent presence in the streetscape.

Inside, the firm developed a sequence of modern Georgian rooms that culminated in Delano's graceful stair that spiraled up to a top-lit dome with bull's-eye windows. A double-height, rusticated entrance vestibule and short stair—recalling that of the Walters Art Gallery—opened up onto the main stair hall, a dynamic, T-shaped space with curved walls at the southern and eastern ends and intersecting ceiling vaults above. Within each of the public rooms, Delano explored variations of attenuated classical order and ensured that each interior was bathed in light by including huge, double-hung windows with sills at the floor and narrow mullions. The abundant light accentuated the profiles of the moldings and relief of the decoration.

Following the Knickerbocker Club commission, the firm executed clubhouses for the Colony Club and The Brook. Aldrich designed the Colony Club's new building at 564 Park Avenue (1914–16) as a reflection of the Colony's original clubhouse at 120 Madison Avenue (1907) designed by Stanford White—the first formal women's club building in New York. The program of Aldrich's eight-story clubhouse was vast; interiors included reception and dining rooms, a library, a double-height ballroom, a loggia, and twenty guest rooms. The building also housed a gymnasium, squash courts, and a pool that, in 1916, was the deepest in the city.[104] Compared to the Knickerbocker Club, Aldrich's Georgian style was more literal than his partner's. The club's Park Avenue facades were applied with a three-bay colossal order of engaged columns and pilasters supporting a full entablature and pediment, while the 62nd Street facade was detailed with a simple overlay of

engaged pilasters. The orders were well proportioned but seemed stretched on the facade, and the building entrance, set in the marble base, had little rhetorical power.

Inside, Aldrich showed his proficiency at designing spatially rich, well-arranged sequences. He successfully buried the functions of the club that did not need light at the building's northwest corner and interleaved the complex layers of mezzanine and double-height spaces. Of the club's rooms, the most spectacular was the loggia with colorful, exotic frescos by Robert Winthrop Chanler that *Vogue* described as "brilliant" and "daring"—"the only temperamental touch . . . permitted by the architects and decorators."[105]

In his city commissions, Delano was also the master of subtle expression. His design for The Brook at 111 East 54th Street (1924–25), a residentially scaled clubhouse, could almost have passed for a private house. Formed as a protest to the Century's early closing hour, the club—named after Lord Tennyson's poem, *The Brook*—was organized in 1903 to be open to members any time of day or night as a convivial alternative to its more polite elder. Delano differentiated the building's severe, planar facades with three reliefs set over the *piano nobile* and a band course carved with dolphins at the entrance level.[106] Its decoration was so subtle and well integrated it might almost have been missed.

Commissions for several large city houses followed the completion of the Knickerbocker Club and, similarly, almost all were carried out in brick. Delano designed a residence for Willard D. Straight at 1130 Fifth Avenue (1913–15) (see pages 104–7) upon his marriage to Dorothy Whitney, the daughter of William C. Whitney, secretary of the navy under Grover Cleveland.[107] Delano met Straight in Havana in 1906 and the two men immediately became close friends. Talented and charismatic, Straight rose to heights in his careers as financier, diplomat, and editor, despite an early death during the influenza epidemic of 1918. Delano's balanced, brick, marble-trimmed corner mansion, on the northernmost point of development along Fifth Avenue, reiterated the architect's skill at creating a pleasing composition of rectilinear lines, inspired by Federal precedent, and Baroque sculpturality, as seen in the house's Wren-inspired attic story windows. The house was built on a grand scale, yet its facades were neither imposing nor overwhelming. Elements of whimsy, such as the wrought-iron peacock set within the front door fanlight, were to become one of the hallmarks of Delano's work.

Delano placed a rotunda-like hall at the center of the plan with vaults leading to public rooms east and west. From this internal rotunda, the main stair landing was bathed in the glow of a skylight above. By framing the first landing, the source of the skylight was obscured from the entry, making the effect mysterious and surprising. Flanking the rotunda were two oval dressing rooms for guests decorated with murals on a naval theme by Howard Gardiner Cushing.

Smaller houses, however, formed the backbone of Delano & Aldrich's city practice. While most were austere brick compositions, the architects' facility for charm and variation distinguished each commission. A reserved Georgian design for Delano's Yale classmate William Sloane, at 686 Park Avenue (1917–19), formed—along with McKim, Mead & White's residences for Percy Pyne (1910–12) and Oliver D. Filey (1926), and Walker & Gillette's for Henry P. Davison (1917)—the city's first blockfront of Colonial Revival buildings.[108] The shallow entrance

WILLARD STRAIGHT HOUSE
Dressing room with murals
by Howard Gardner Cushing
Patterson, *American Homes of To-day*

WILLIAM SLOANE HOUSE
686 Park Avenue, New York City

Architectural Review 8 [1919]: pl. 11. Courtesy of Avery Architectural and Fine Arts Library, Columbia University in the City of New York

portico, supported by Corinthian columns, gave the facade presence while decorative window grilles of shell and floral motifs, stone lintels, and rounded dormers lent it vitality.

For financier and civic leader, R. Fulton Cutting, the firm designed a family enclave on East 88th and 89th Streets (1919–22) that consisted of four townhouses.[109] The three houses that fronted 89th Street were rigorously restrained and blended together as if it were one large building. A first-floor arcade hiding the service stairs unified the front facade and relieved the severity of the design; the house on 89th Street backed against a communal garden shared by all four houses. A later house for banker Harry Rogers Winthrop at 120 East 78th Street (1930), inspired by Thomas Jefferson's pavilions at the University of Virginia, was a unique interpretation by the firm of a New York City townhouse facade. The Winthrop house's principal facade was dominated by a recessed colossal niche, painted white, inset with a curved stair running up to the front entrance.

A great mansard roof perforated with bull's-eye windows, pedimented dormers, and massive chimneys animated Delano's brick and stone residence for financier Francis Palmer at 75 East 93rd Street (1917) (see pages 132–35).[110] When George F. Baker, Jr., heir to the First National City Bank fortune, purchased the house in 1928, he commissioned Delano to add a ballroom wing, a garage, and a four-story house for his father around the original house. Delano, in turn, created a quiet complex centered around a walled garden overlooking 93rd Street, skillfully knitting together the three distinct facades with classical, as well as whimsical, details, marble trim, and a belt course carved with chain-links at the attic story.

Delano's limestone and marble residence for William Woodward, president of the National Hanover Bank, at 9 East 86th Street (1916–18) (see pages 122–25) was a particularly chaste design built on a grand scale.[111] By carving out space within the composition for a one-story entrance pavilion and terrace, Delano cleverly gave the mid-block house the appearance of a freestanding building. As it had in the Knickerbocker Club design, Delano's gesture lent variety to the building and enabled light to filter into the second layer of rooms. Inside, the main hall led to a huge, top-lit gallery containing one of Delano's few rectangular stairs. At the top, a frieze was suggested by a band of plaster-swag, framed portraits of the twelve Caesars.

Harold I. Pratt's residence at 60 East 68th Street (1919–20) (see pages 136–39) was equally impressive.[112] Compositionally, the house resembled the Straight residence with the exception of the door placement. Despite this variation, both residences were composed of a large center hall crossing the house with primary rooms opening on either side. Capped by skylights, the center stairs served only the entertaining rooms on the second floor; the space carved out of the building mass above created interior light courts and allowed for more windows on the upper floors. Delano dressed the Pratt house in limestone and marble, rather than brick, and incorporated octagonal attic-story windows and dolphin-and-shell friezes.

Delano & Aldrich's city houses and clubs exhibited the architects' ability to play with space and detail, giving rise to an array of remarkably inventive designs. In comparison, the firm's school buildings—most of which were designed by Aldrich—were much more reserved. However, in their design the firm continued to demonstrate its unwavering faith in simple form and pure proportion. St. Bernard's at

4 East 98th Street (1915) was a rigorous five-bay, brick block accented with lime-stone trim and a shallow entrance portico. Aldrich's Kips Bay Boys Club at 301–307 East 52nd Street (1930) was a severe, seven-bay building with minimal trim. His designs for Miss Chapin's School at 100 East End Avenue (1927–28) and the Nightingale-Bamford School at 20 East 92nd Street (1929) were slightly less stringent; the severity of their planar facades was offset by more varied window patterns. Overlooking Carl Schurz Park and the East River, Miss Chapin's was a comfortable, five-story building with arched windows, limestone base and belt courses, and bay windows framing the composition on the upper stories. The principal facade of the Nightingale-Bamford brick school building was animated by four double-height, arched windows on the *piano nobile* flanked by two octagonal bull's-eyes.[113]

The design of the five-bay Greenwich Settlement House at 29 Barrow Street (1916–17), also by Aldrich, recalled that of the Colony Club and displayed the architect's propensity for applied ornament. The building, capped with a balustrade and a steeply pitched roof, was embellished with stone panels at the attic story and medallions modeled by Gertrude Vanderbilt Whitney. Like Delano's studio for Whitney, the Greenwich Settlement House was an artistic collaboration. Whitney, vice-president of the organization, and Aldrich were interested in fostering awareness of the arts; rooms were handsomely decorated and painted by Augustus Vincent Tack, Eugene Savage, and Arthur Crisp.[114] Aldrich subsequently designed

an arts-and-crafts and music building for Greenwich House nearby to serve the neighborhood children.

The Union Club at 701 Park Avenue (1927–33) (see pages 148–55) was the last major private city project the firm undertook.[115] The club sold its old building at the height of the real-estate market, and the proceeds provided an unusually abundant budget during the depths of the Depression. The Union was considerably different from the firm's Federal brick clubhouses; Delano was at the mercy of the club's building committee, who instructed the architect to evoke the style of its ornate Fifth Avenue building by Cass Gilbert and John Du Fais. Delano bridled at this direction but managed to deliver a superb building with modern touches. The scale of the clubhouse, containing a vast program, was great; its granite facades were muscularly rusticated and detailed.

Inside, Delano created a refreshing balance between iconic form and his modern interpretation of classical vocabulary. The interiors were exuberantly detailed with bold lanterns and chandeliers and stylized moldings, mantels, and consoles reflecting the purpose of the room. In the most traditional of forums, Delano's spirited brand of classicism abounded. The Union Club was the last great building the firm was to complete in Manhattan and its design may very well be considered a turning point for Delano & Aldrich. After the Depression, as the firm moved toward an architecture increasingly *moderne* and distilled, the Union Club stood as one of the most discernable designs linking the firm's traditional, residentially scaled buildings and clubhouses to its later, more diversified, large-scale projects.

While Delano generally disapproved of tall buildings, he was forthright in his praise of the collaborative efforts of the architect and engineer. He wrote:

> Today, with steel, we have almost limitless possibilities, and the Woolworth and Bush Terminal buildings stand as monuments to the skill of their designers and the times. I venture to say that these buildings, expressions of modern problems, have awakened many emotions in the hearts of the beholders as most cathedrals. Haven't you been thrilled by them as you beheld them soaring into space, whether in broad daylight or as twilight gathered or as night fell? I know I have.[116]

Delano's admiration for skyscrapers was reserved for an inspired few. Coolidge, Shepley, Bulfinch & Abbott's New York Hospital (1934) embodied for Delano the best of New York skyscraper design, "a happy combination of tradition, expressed in modern form, simple in composition."[117] However, he felt strongly that most skyscrapers were scaled to capitalize on limited space rather than to sustain the dignity of human life and, en masse, they were hedging in the city streets, creating congestion, traffic, and "canyons without sunlight and air."[118] Delano believed that "size has little to do with great Architecture. A small structure which solves the problem perfectly may well awaken as keen an emotion as a vast one."[119]

The firm did design one prominently located New York skyscraper for the banking house of Brown Brothers & Company (1927–29) (see pages 144–47).[120] Delano's design for the bank's 37-story tower, set on an irregular lot bound by Wall, Hanover, and William Streets, was inspired, strongly detailed, and dynamic. Like New York Hospital, completed five years later, the Brown Brothers building was composed to address the challenge of bringing proportion, harmony, and balance to an oversized modern type. The building's three-story limestone base was decorated with fluted piers, stylized spandrels, and medallions based on ancient coins; the tower, an intricate carved mass indented to bring light to the center of each floor, was treated separately from the base and embellished with brickwork spandrels, narrow piers, and limestone accents. With oblong bull's-eye windows and gargoyles, the roofline was set apart from those of other office buildings on Wall Street. This adroit exercise in massing showed that the firm was capable of understanding the tall urban building in the context of both the street and the larger cityscape.

The firm's commission for the Brown Brothers & Company building led to an important project in Cincinnati—the Carew Tower and Netherland Plaza Complex (1930–1931), an innovative, mixed-use facility developed by John J. Emery and designed by Walter W. Ahlschlager of Chicago. Having completed Emery's Indian Hill estate one year earlier, Delano & Aldrich was called onto the project to develop the tower's massing. Like the Brown Brothers & Company tower, the 48-story skyscraper had a strong limestone base and a rising shaft composed of a series of setbacks with stylized classical details.[121]

Although they were working in a city where development was soaring, Delano and Aldrich held fast to their preferred métier and produced few designs for loft or apartment buildings. Early commercial buildings for Henry Barbey at 15 West 38th Street (1908) and music publisher G. Schirmer at 7 East 43rd Street (1909) illustrated the architects' struggle with the new building type and displayed a more lit-

BROWN BROTHERS & COMPANY
59–63 Wall Street, New York City

John Wallace Gillies. Delano & Aldrich Collection, Avery Architectural and Fine Arts Library, Columbia University in the City of New York

eral reading of precedent. The twelve-story brick Barbey Building was awkwardly composed of one bay extending the height of the building capped by an elaborate Baroque scroll and urns.[122] Delano's seven-story building for music publisher G. Schirmer was more coherent. The building's cornice barely projected, yet the roofline was finished with attic-story bull's-eyes, French detail, and urns. Lyres in bas relief referred to the building's commercial purposes.[123]

Aldrich's 925 Park Avenue (1907–9) was one of the first luxury apartment buildings to be constructed on the regenerated avenue. McKim, Mead & White's 998 Fifth Avenue and Warren & Wetmore's 903 Park Avenue, two of the Upper East Side's most luxurious buildings, were completed in 1912. Aldrich's fourteen-floor limestone and terracotta palazzo was composed of upper-story duplexes and three triplexes accessible to the street. A mixture of Italian and French influences, the building had a rusticated base marked by two-story arches encompassing both apartment windows and entrances. Aldrich attempted to add character to the design with French grille work and a bold cartouche, elements that seem overwhelmed by the inflated scale of the building.[124]

Delano's 1040 Park Avenue (1923–25) was a more refined and elegant modern classical design.[125] With its whimsical third-story frieze of tortoise and hare figures capping its base, the building facades were articulated by angled vertical ribs formed by projecting bricks that ran from the base to the attic story where they connected with an understated frieze of shells and triglyphs. The building originally contained three spacious apartments per floor, and Condé Nast's 30-room penthouse occupied the building's rooftop space as well as one of the three top-floor apartments, which was reworked for bedroom space. Additional servants' quarters had originally been designed for the roof. However, in 1924, before the upper floors of the building were constructed, plans changed to include Nast's apartment. Decorated by Elsie de Wolfe, Nast's apartment centered on a 43-foot ballroom and glass conservatory in which Nast entertained extravagantly.

Aldrich's twelve-story chapter house for the American Red Cross at 315 Lexington Avenue (1929) continued the firm's exploration of expressive brickwork. The brick composition was enlivened by a strongly articulated *piano nobile* accented with French windows, grille work, and intricately molded brick details.[126]

PUBLIC BUILDINGS

OPPOSITE

THIRD CHURCH OF CHRIST
SCIENTIST
583 Park Avenue, New York City

Paul J. Weber. Delano & Aldrich Collection,
Avery Architectural and Fine Arts Library,
Columbia University in the City of New York

Given its architectural fluency and powerful connections, Delano & Aldrich was, unlike many other firms, able to make the transition from residential to public work to meet the architectural demands of the 1930s and 1940s. With the onset of the Depression, the era of grand country estates and city houses came to an abrupt halt, but through luck, effort, and agility the partners were able to keep their draftsmen employed. Delano energetically sought out work for his office, successfully keeping his devoted team intact until new commissions were won. At one low point, the firm's draftsmen were kept busy designing and constructing dollhouses for Macy's Department Store. Available in three different models—brick colonial, stucco, or city house—they sold for $10 to $12.[127]

During the first decades of their partnership, Delano and Aldrich designed an incredible array of churches, school buildings, hospitals, galleries, and banks, rounding out their residential practice. The scope and variety of this work was considerable; the architects even succumbed to working in more picturesque styles, which they had hitherto tried to avoid. The public and institutional projects completed during this period provided a concrete basis for the firm's larger, more comprehensive projects and airport commissions to come.

Delano & Aldrich entered many civic competitions, but invariably lost the prize. In 1948, Delano contemplated his frequent defeat by John Russell Pope: "Apart from his ability as an architect, Jack had an uncanny way of reading the minds of juries, in the many competitions in which we both took part. Jack, with his able assistants, always walked away with the prize."[128] In fact, the firm did not win a major competition until 1944, when it won the Expansion Program at West Point.

In the 1930s, Delano & Aldrich's practice shifted almost entirely to public and governmental work. Despite Aldrich's departure from the firm in 1935 for the Academy of Rome and Delano's declining health—a result of several unsuccessful back operations that left him partially crippled—the firm completed several important projects during this time, culminating in the commission for New York's Municipal Airport (1937–42) and Delano's appointment as architectural consultant to the Commission on the Renovation of the White House (1949–52). The 1930s and 1940s did hold several disappointments: World War II thwarted plans for an addition to London's National Gallery (1939–40) and two major projects, Idlewild Airport (1945) and the Expansion Program for West Point (1945), sat unresolved for several years before eventually being called off in the late 1940s.[129] While the firm continued under the auspices of "Delano & Aldrich" until the mid 1950s, the last public work to come out of the office under Delano's stewardship was the Epinal American Cemetery and Memorial for the American Battle Monuments Commission in Epinal, France (1948–56). Delano retired from the firm in 1949 and assumed the role of advisory partner on January 1, 1950.

CHURCHES

Delano & Aldrich's freestanding churches were executed exclusively in variations of the Georgian mode.[130] New York's Third Church of Christ Scientist at 583 Park Avenue (1922–24) was the only church the firm built in New York and was its most ambitious ecclesiastical venture. The design, a sophisticated square brick and limestone edifice, recalled Stanford White's Madison Square Presbyterian Church (1906), a building with which Delano must have been familiar since his grandfather was once its parson. While White's church was a richly polychromed, full-bodied classical monument, both buildings were organized around the Greek cross plan with domes and boldly scaled porticos. Although, in comparison, Delano & Aldrich's facades were pared down, it was that very economy that reinforced the building's presence on the avenue, especially when juxtaposed with the neighboring Gothic Park Avenue Baptist Church (1922) by Henry C. Pelton and Allen & Collens. The church's two-story entrance portico was supported by four colossal Ionic columns, and the building was capped by an intricate wrought-iron lantern decorated with urns. The stark white nave, with mahogany trim and unadorned buff-colored walls, contained exquisite, architect-designed chandeliers built by Foster Gunnison and was surmounted by a coffered dome and oculus.[131]

DUTCH REFORMED CHURCH
Brookville, New York

Delano & Aldrich Collection, #74899,
Collection of the New-York Historical Society

While the Third Church of Christ Scientist, according to Aldrich, "was designed to follow the style of an old-fashioned New England Meeting House of the Eighteenth Century," Delano came closer to achieving this austere ambiance with his chaste Georgian design for the Brookville Dutch Reformed Church (1924).[132] Howard Robertson of *Architecture and Building* pronounced the white stucco, spired church "more of an architectural achievement than the Christian Scientist Church" with "the advantage of setting, freer groupings, and unity of color." Robertson felt the "design capture[d] an atmosphere of dignity and even richness which [was] all in a rustic and unsophisticated key."[133] Delano's Wren-inspired church was perhaps more severe than its Puritan and Federal antecedents; in the eighteenth century, builders and townspeople reveled in the delicate wooden ornament that might set their meetinghouse or church apart, whereas Delano's design delighted in its absence.

Delano & Aldrich designed several Gothic and Romanesque church extensions, parsonages, and education buildings. However, they carried out designs in a more picturesque style only when the context of the commission called for its use. Alterations and additions to Christ Church in Hartford, Connecticut (1916–17); Westminster Presbyterian Church in Albany, New York (1928–30); and Crescent Avenue Presbyterian Church in Plainfield, New Jersey (1930–31) showed that the architects were capable of working in the Gothic style.[134]

School Buildings and Campuses

The firm's institutional commissions also showed leanings toward contextualism. Several of Delano's buildings at Yale, executed during the 1910s and 1920s, were modern Gothic hybrids sympathetic with James Gamble Rogers's collegiate Gothic campus.[135] Willard Straight Hall at Cornell (1923–25), one of the country's first student unions and situated next to the university's oldest Gothic school buildings, was also carried out in a modern Gothic mode and contained a large theater with murals painted by J. Monroe Hewlett.[136] Willard Straight's widow, Dorothy Whitney Straight, commissioned the union as a memorial to her husband who had received a degree in architecture from Cornell School of Architecture.

Delano & Aldrich's Gothic syntax, however, could be stripped to the essentials and blended with French or Georgian undertones. The Sterling Chemistry Laboratory (1921–23) was a stunning example of Delano's ability to combine disparate traditions to create a fluid and functional design. At first glance, the large laboratory on Prospect Hill appeared as a rambling fortress rising majestically above New Haven. However, the sprawling picturesque quality of the building was deceiving; in actuality, the laboratory was tightly and rationally organized, its interior space divided into three sections: lecture rooms, research rooms, and a general area for student laboratory work. A sawtooth roof structure allowed flexibility within the interiors; the general spaces could be subdivided into classrooms by moving non-bearing partitions. The laboratory's center doorway, surmounted by a great Gothic transom window, punctuated the building's symmetrical front facade, which, with few windows, was textured with vertical piers and dentils etched with the symbols for the elements of the periodic table; classical lanterns emphasized the corners of the building. While the building retained qualities of the Gothic, elements such as severe brick walls, classical lanterns, symmetry, and legible plan recalled the Beaux-Arts.[137] As Bertram Grosvenor Goodhue, himself a reluctant

TOP

SMITH COLLEGE MUSIC SCHOOL
(SAGE HALL)
Northampton, Massachusetts

Paul J. Weber. Delano & Aldrich Collection,
Avery Architectural and Fine Arts Library,
Columbia University in the City of New York

ABOVE

STERLING DIVINITY SCHOOL
*Yale University, New Haven,
Connecticut*

Photographs of Sterling Divinity Quadrangle,
Yale University [RU 628]. Manuscripts and Archives,
Yale University Library

practitioner of the English Gothic, once said to Delano, "Bill, what I like about the laboratory of yours is that it is not too *damn* Gothic."[138]

In most cases, the firm did not submit to the "prevailing Gothic madness" in school architecture.[139] Aldrich's Music School at Smith College (1923–26) was a brick and limestone edifice capped with a raised dome punctuated by bull's-eyes, reminiscent of Jefferson's dome at Monticello, and embellished by a entrance portico supported by elegant Ionic columns.[140] Delano & Aldrich's campuses for The Lawrenceville School in Lawrenceville, New Jersey, The Hotchkiss School in Lakeville, Connecticut, and the Sterling Divinity School at Yale were carried out in the firm's typically restrained interpretation of the Georgian style—or what Delano described as his "own expression of the simplest and most straightforward facades that would solve the problem."[141] Although Delano was reluctant to assign stylistic labels to his work, he often called attention to the time-honored, traditional models from which he drew inspiration. In speaking of Yale, Delano remarked, "I have been accused in this of copying the University of Virginia, and I am proud of it, for the University of Virginia was copied by Jefferson from the plan of Marly and that, in turn, doubtless from a Roman villa: only today, architects' designs spring fullfledged from the head of the designer."[142] While the Yale Divinity School (1930–32) (see pages 170–73) followed its precedent more closely than Delano's other school designs, all three campuses were modeled loosely on the Jeffersonian ideal of the "academic village."

"Though they lean heavily on Mr. Jefferson's university at Charlottesville," Lewis Mumford conceded that the Yale buildings did "show the possibilities of small units in school design."[143] Delano's campus was broken into three distinct, yet fluid, spaces for residential, learning, and communal purposes. Like Jefferson's

design, there were no freestanding buildings; the six dormitory pavilions, class-room, and communal buildings were connected by arcades and hyphens and con-verged at the central, Wren-inspired chapel.[144] Delano ingeniously designed the campus for its hillside site. Through the play of site levels, he stressed the vertical-ity of the chapel, at the crest of the incline, in relation to the dormitories, and by wrapping the composition around the back of the chapel, he was able to create a secondary green to the rear and to mask the size of the larger buildings housing communal spaces.

While the Sterling Divinity School was the most comprehensive campus Delano designed, his plans for The Lawrenceville School (1922–37) also exhibited the architect's aptitude for organizing space. As the semi-official school architect, Delano designed seven buildings for his alma mater over a period of fifteen years, creating a secondary campus within the school, an adjunct to Frederick Law Olmsted's original layout. Delano's buildings were formally grouped around a sunken garden, known as the Bowl; the Fathers' Building, the large pedimented classroom building at the head of the lawn, anchored a strong axis along which Delano's dormitories, administration building, and small library were organized; the dialogue between those buildings created secondary axes across the green.[145]

At the same time, the firm was also working at Hotchkiss, a feeder school for Yale, founded in 1891. Over a span of more than twenty years (1929–52), Delano & Aldrich added two dormitories, a dining hall, chapel, entrance gates, and library to the school's centralized campus that also included buildings by Bruce Price and Cass Gilbert. Tightly organized around a main axis, the school buildings formed an ensemble distinct from the firm's gymnasium complex designed for a site across the street. In characteristic manner, Delano & Aldrich's work exhibited the possibilities

MONAHAN GYMNASIUM
The Hotchkiss School
Lakeville, Connecticut

Courtesy of The Hotchkiss School,
Lakeville, Connecticut

PHILADELPHIA ORPHANAGE
Wallingford, Pennsylvania

Delano & Aldrich Collection,
Avery Architectural and Fine Arts Library,
Columbia University in the City of New York

of brick as an ornamental feature. The chapel, a spare rectilinear building capped by a lantern, was composed of bricks molded and patterned to evoke the elements of classical language—even triglyphs and swags. The main facade of Monahan gymnasium was punctuated with a monumental recessed entrance niche and textured with brick dentils, spandrel panels, and limestone medallions depicting athletes; the simplicity of the design was powerful and elegant.[146]

HOSPITALS AND ORPHANAGES

As a precursor to their campus plans, the Philadelphia Orphanage in Wallingford, Pennsylvania (1904–5), displayed Delano & Aldrich's facility, at an early stage, for planning a self-contained community. The firm acquired the orphanage commission in 1904 after winning a limited competition. Their Georgian brick and white wood–trimmed scheme with landscaped gardens was situated on a level plot in rural Pennsylvania. The H-shaped plan organized the program: girls and boys' accommodations, dining rooms, and classrooms occupied the oblong wings while the administration was housed in the central section of the building. Arcades, extending out of the wings, connected an isolation hospital and a laundry; formal gardens were designed to fill the interstices. The two-story building created a warm and comfortable environment for the children and, according to *The New York Architect,* "as a whole [had] a domestic rather than institutional character."[147]

While the firm designed a series of utilitarian structures in Newfoundland for
the International Grenfell Association, its hospitals in more fashionable and visible
locales were treated more architecturally.[148] Delano & Aldrich's Private Patients'
Pavilion at the Flower Hospital in New York City (c. 1914), executed in a stripped
Georgian idiom with stone trim, was also domestically scaled, reminiscent more of
the firm's larger city houses and clubs. The facility, intended for wealthy and dis-
criminating patients, contained a series of bedrooms with private baths and fire-
places.[149] Similarly, Aldrich's Austin Riggs Foundation (1930) in Stockbridge,
Massachusetts, was designed in the spirit of Delano & Aldrich's local houses.[150] The
two-story, white brick building with symmetrical wings housed the private psychi-
atric facility where patients were thought to benefit from an open residential setting.

SMALL PUBLIC BUILDINGS

Delano & Aldrich's public work prior to the 1930s was typically small in scale and
privately funded. The Cushing Memorial Art Gallery in Newport, Rhode Island
(1919–20), was a charming and intimate museum designed in tribute to Delano's
friend and colleague the artist Howard Gardiner Cushing. Delano and Cushing had
worked together on a number of projects, including Willard Straight's house in
New York and Gertrude Vanderbilt Whitney's studio on Long Island, where
Cushing painted exotic murals for the dressing rooms (Straight) and stair hall
(Whitney); the firm had also designed his New York residence on East 70th Street.
The design of the Palladian gallery recalled that of Whitney's studio, carried out on
a smaller scale and with a more reserved touch. But, despite its diminutive size, the
building had a noble stature. The detail on the facades' crisp, clean surfaces was
minimal; only the round entrance portico with its black marble columns and gilt
bronze capitals and the stone quoins interrupted the smooth, stucco surfaces.[151]

STATEN ISLAND SAVINGS BANK
Staten Island, New York

Raymond A. Warrender.
Delano & Aldrich Collection,
Avery Architectural and Fine Arts Library,
Columbia University in the City of New York

Aldrich's Staten Island Savings Bank (1923–24) was also a sturdy Italian Renaissance–inspired building, executed in Indiana limestone. On a thin, irregular site, the bank was anchored by a single-story, rusticated base around the bank's central space, a double-height elliptical hall with a mezzanine level that displayed six arched windows, a skylight, and a cerulean blue dome. A circular portico, similar to that of the Cushing gallery, marked the bank's main entrance at the corner of the building and was capped with a cast-lead dome patterned with a fish-scale design. The sea motif was reiterated in the design of the fish-shaped exterior lanterns.[152]

OTHER WORKS

Working in collaboration with engineers, Delano & Aldrich executed two bridges (1923–24) for the Bronx Parkway Commission as part of a viaduct system. Constructed along the parkway's scenic grounds at river crossings or at graded intersections, the bridges enabled the parkway to run continuously, a novel concept in the 1910s and 1920s when there were few roads that extended at length uninterrupted by intersections or stoplights. The bridges were designed using the latest engineering developments in steel and reinforced concrete and were faced with native stone to harmonize with the natural setting and rock outcrops along the highway.

At the time of its construction, Delano & Aldrich's bridge #28 at Scarsdale was considered a unique structural solution raising the parkway over the picturesque Scarsdale Lake and the tracks of the New York Central Railroad. A single line of eight reinforced-concrete "mushroom units" enhanced by structural brackets and fascias raised the viaduct over the lake, and a plate-girder span, faced in paneled concrete, carried the drive over the tracks. Although Delano & Aldrich's work for the Bronx Parkway Commission was somewhat atypical, the architects valued modern materials and techniques and supported a close collaboration between architect and engineer.[153]

After the onset of the Depression, Delano completed the Lauxmont Dairy in Wrightsville, Pennsylvania (1932–33), on the estate of S. Forry Laucks. In addition to the dairy, Delano & Aldrich also built a stone manor overlooking the Susquehanna River for Laucks as well as a sizable munitions plant during World War II in York, Pennsylvania, for the York Safe and Lock Company of which Laucks was president.[154] While the firm had considerable expertise in designing farm groups for country estates, the Lauxmont Dairy was a larger facility with advanced equipment and methods for dairy farming. In this innovative facility, the cows were milked in a separate room or "milking parlor" instead of in their pens, and the milking machines were operated by vacuum. Pens were arranged in a U-shaped fashion around a grass court with the milking parlor and its accompanying observation rooms located at the head.

Constructed of stuccoed block walls and slag roofs, the farm structures were spare. Almost abstract in articulation, the group's plain white facades were punctuated by horizontal windows, attenuated louvered vents, and circular or octagonal

S. FORRY LAUCKS DAIRY FARM
Lauxmont Dairy
Wrightsville, Pennsylvania

Robert W. Tebbs. *Architectural Record* 76 [September 1934]: 194. Courtesy of Avery Architectural and Fine Arts Library, Columbia University in the City of New York

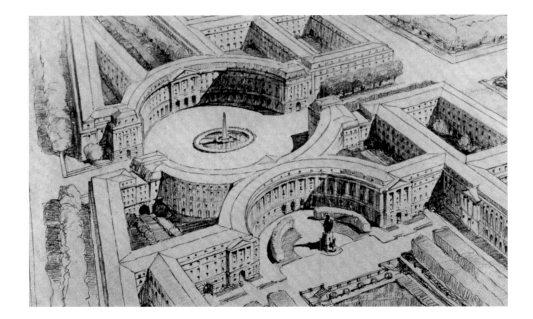

AS PLANNED: UNITED STATES
POST OFFICE DEPARTMENT
BUILDING AND CIRCULAR PLAZA
Washington, D.C.
Rendering by Chester B. Price

bull's-eyes, and the roofs were arched or dramatically pitched. With little architectural differentiation, the buildings were distinguished more by adroit massing and their distinct forms. The main barn bore a striking resemblance to Delano's design for the Harrison Williams's tennis court building as the architects maintained their facility for translating fundamental forms to express disparate building types.

Government Work

Delano's appointment by President Coolidge to the National Commission of Fine Arts (1924–28) signaled the beginning of a twenty-eight-year involvement with Washington, D.C. and led to other appointments and commissions within the capital city and abroad. With his foot in the door, Delano was subsequently invited to join the Board of Architectural Consultants (1927–33), the group of architects responsible for designing the Federal Triangle, and the National Capital Parks and Planning Commission (1929–46), a committee responsible for planning and zoning the capital.[155] While working in Washington, Delano befriended several of Washington's key players, including Andrew Mellon, then secretary of the Treasury; Ulysses S. Grant, superintendent of Buildings and Grounds; and Keith Merrill, secretary of the Foreign Service Building Commission. These associations led to commissions for the Japanese Embassy (1930–31) and the American Government Building in Paris (1929–32), two of Delano's favorite projects, as well as a new roof and a third story for the White House (1927).

Of Delano & Aldrich's government projects, the United State Post Office Department Building and Circular Plaza for the Federal Triangle (1928–35) (see pages 158–63) was the most ambitious.[156] Delano's building formed an integral part of Washington's massive urban redevelopment program, and his involvement in the highly visible, much anticipated project showed his mastery of the public scale. Each of the architects on the Board of Architectural Consultants, appointed by

AS PLANNED: UNITED STATES
POST OFFICE DEPARTMENT
BUILDING AND CIRCULAR PLAZA
Washington, D.C.
Rendering by Chester B. Price

Architectural Forum 55 [September 1931]: 263.
Courtesy of Avery Architectural and Fine Arts
Library, Columbia University in the City
of New York

Andrew Mellon, was allotted one building in the Triangle to design. The seven-member committee was composed of classically trained architects, and the National Commission of Fine Arts, on which Delano also served, collaborated on the overall design. They created a cohesive seven-building group with a fixed cornice height of 105 feet based on Pierre Charles L'Enfant's formalized conception of 1791 and the subsequent McMillan plan.[157]

Mellon proposed that the buildings, while "having each a separate and distinctive architectural treatment, [should] be of harmonious design and grouped around two large interior courts of plazas somewhat after the arrangement of the Louvre in Paris."[158] Given the architectural composition of the board, it was not surprising that the monumental limestone buildings of the Triangle were muscularly rusticated and clearly Beaux-Arts–inspired. The connection between the buildings was immediate; they moved directly into one another, fusing into one distinct ensemble. The triangle easily embodied the qualities Delano considered fundamental to an American public building: "more monumental than the ordinary commercial building or private house. A sense of volume, the relationship of the voids to the solids, a possible overemphasis of certain parts, all contribute to give this quality of building, but the most essential are proportion and an appearance of enduring stability."[159] Delano regretted that his arcaded hemicycle was never completed; the old Romanesque post office on the northwest corner of the site was never razed as originally intended. However, his contribution and the public space it created was championed by Henry Hope Reed as "the only square of its kind in the country and, despite its present disposition, one of which the nation should be proud."[160]

Concurrently, Delano & Aldrich was also working on the American Government Building (1929–32) (see pages 164–69) on the Place de la Concorde, Paris's original royal square designed by Jacques-Ange Gabriel.[161] Replacing a 1769 mansion that did not conform to the regulations governing Gabriel's plan, Delano's new building completed the tetrad of buildings, consisting of the Hôtel Crillon, the Ministry of the Navy, and the Hôtel Talleyrand, along the square's northern edge.

The building's well-proportioned facades, common roofline, and complementary relationship of solids and voids fulfilled its contextual spirit on the historic square. Delano established a dialogue with the adjacent buildings by extending the axis created by the grand arcade through a side gate into the Chancellery's front garden. At the same time, the building was given an American identity; its facades were decorated unobtrusively with American seals and eagles. Like the interiors at the United States Post Office Department Building and the Union Club, the rooms were furnished with an endearing twist of classical and Deco motifs.

During the same period, Delano & Aldrich was willing to bend to the wishes of a foreign government and returned to the Georgian-inspired vernacular characteristic of its country houses when the firm designed the Japanese Embassy (1930–31) in Washington, D.C. Its design was smaller in scale and more modest than the firm's work at the Federal Triangle and in Paris. The formal composition of the embassy and its dependencies was more reminiscent of the firm's Beaux-Arts estates than its grander designs for government buildings.[162]

Delano & Aldrich's work became markedly more distilled by the mid-1930s. Aldrich's contribution to the design for a new ferry house at Ellis Island (1933–36), constructed under the New Deal's Public Works Administration, gave rise to a crisp, symmetrical, brick building decorated with abstract limestone bands articulating shifts in elevation.[163] The firm's Works Progress Administration building designed for the 1939 World's Fair, also a modern classical building, was even more pared down.

Delano served on the fair's Board of Design (1936–39) under Grover A. Whalen, president of the Fair Corporation, with Stephen F. Voorhees (Chairman), Gilmore D. Clarke, Jay Downer, Robert D. Kohn, Walter Dorwin Teague and Richmond H. Shreve. Known as the "WORLD OF TOMORROW," the fair had a futuristic pitch. The board was responsible for developing the general plan and overseeing all of the fair's design aspects. While the architecture was, for the most part, streamlined and modernistic, the Board's master plan was more classically inspired, allowing for clear axes and visual coherence.[164]

Harrison & Foulihoux's Theme Center, the so-called Trylon and Perisphere, was the centerpiece. The geometric purity of its giant sphere and elongated spike—unleavened by classical language—made the Trylon and Perisphere an icon of heroic modernism. In his role as board member, Delano had to comment on Harrison's design. Harmon Goldstone, then a young architect in the Harrison office, was apprehensive: "We were worried because the design board consisted of establishment architects and the sphere and triangle were far out . . . The last man to come was William Delano; we were all scared of him. He was the height of conventionality, a gent of the old school. We were amazed how quickly he got the aesthetic of what we were trying to do. He was so sensitive to proportion and design; the lack of columns and pedestals didn't bother him at all. He gave the most solid and subtle criticism regarding the proper height of the sphere from the water, which we took into account at once."[165]

The power of Delano & Aldrich's stripped classical form was even more pronounced at the Epinal American Cemetery and Memorial (1948–56), one of fourteen World War II monuments constructed abroad by the American Battle Monuments Commission.[166] The complex, located in the remote foothills of France's Vosges Mountains, was composed of a visitor's building and a monumental white stone memorial housing a small chapel and museum and embellished with bas-relief sculpture by Malvina Hoffman. With its stark symmetry, stout proportions, and largely clean, undecorated surfaces, Delano's design adhered to the stylistic regulations which were set by the American Battle Monuments Commission based on Paul Cret's interpretation of a new monumental architecture.[167] Facades were elegant and powerful; their crisp lines, refined cornices, and stripped-down columns stood starkly against the greenery and the organization of the landscaping; together, the colors of the grass, white stone, and red flourishes set into the bas-relief were striking. The memorial and the 5,252 white marble headstones, set within the quiet, landscaped cemetery, created a poignant and transporting environment.

THE WHITE HOUSE
Washington, D.C.

South Portico

Abbie Rowe. *Journal of the A.I.A.* 9 [June 1948]:
270. Courtesy of Avery Architectural and
Fine Arts Library, Columbia University in the
City of New York

Although Delano retired from the firm in 1949, he continued to work as the architectural consultant to the Commission on the Renovation of the Executive Mansion until 1952. With his presidency, Harry S. Truman instigated several changes to the White House, including an addition of a second floor balcony within the south portico (1948) and a major structural renovation. The balcony caused a stir within the architectural community. Many, including the National Commission of Fine Arts, felt that such an exterior addition would mar the historic house; Truman was highly criticized for proceeding with the project.[168] Delano, working with White House architect Lorenzo S. Winslow, placed the balcony unobtrusively behind the portico's colonnade and replaced the awkward fixed canopies with less conspicuous retractable awnings. During Truman's extensive renovation, interiors were dismantled and reinstalled within a new steel frame while the exterior walls of the house were retained; Delano oversaw the interior architecture. However, at the age of 75, Delano was drained by the frequent trips to Washington and was often frustrated by the project. Nonetheless, the post shows that Delano was esteemed within his field and by the nation. And although Delano acted only in an advisory capacity, it was the authority of *his* name that carried the project through to a successful end. He could not have left his profession on a higher note.

AIRPORTS

Though the prestigious White House position has been called the culminating event in Delano's career, it was in the realm of airport design that the firm excelled during the later years of its tenure. The 1930s was the golden age of flying, a time when aviation was just developing and flying was considered glamorous and adventuresome. As airport design was relatively undefined, architects and engineers confronted novel problems from infrastructure to basic planning and circulation. Equal to the challenges the evolving industry presented, Delano & Aldrich quickly rose to prominence. While it is surprising that a firm which, up until 1929, was entrenched in house and club design was able to master the uncharted field of airport design, the same Beaux-Arts principles and reliance on pure form helped the firm solve these new problems.

In 1928, Delano & Aldrich designed Pan American Airways System's first terminal in Miami at 36th Street on the site of the current Miami International Airport.[169] Juan Trippe had founded the company a year earlier with the vision of linking the Americas by a single airway carrying mail and passengers. He was awarded the first international mail contract between Florida and Cuba. Delano & Aldrich's terminal operated briefly as the airway's international headquarters.

The design of Delano & Aldrich's two-story, concrete and stucco landplane-seaplane terminal at 36th Street combined simple construction with innovative planning ideas. While the building's architectural expression was rudimentary, the terminal, according to *The American Architect*, was the first "completely equipped station built in America."[170] Its double-height, light-filled atrium was divided in half by Spanish wrought-iron grille work to separate incoming and outgoing passengers, and each section was connected to airplanes by a canopied promenade. The ticket and baggage offices were located on the outgoing side; immigration, customs, and baggage examination on the incoming; and dining rooms, offices, and observation terraces on the second floor. These innovations were cited by aviation historians who considered the Pan American terminal to be one of the earliest "airports" in the United States.[171] Within this industrial, hangar-like building, it is clear that its architects succeeded in facilitating direct circulation through the terminal.[172]

To accommodate the expanding industry, Delano & Aldrich's second seaplane base for Pan American at Miami's Dinner Key (1931–34) was capable of handling four airplanes and 400 people simultaneously. Delano regarded the commission as a "simple problem for never more than two or three planes reached this base at any one time and the only difficulty was to shepherd each shipload through the intricacies of immigration, health, customs, etc., with the least confusion and provide a restaurant with observation terrace."[173] Though the Dinner Key facility was more commodious, its terminal plan was simply an enlarged version of the Miami station; waiting rooms and governmental offices occupied the main floor, and dining rooms and observation terraces the second story. Two passenger ramps with retractable canopies led from either side of the building at the basement level out to the Clippers floating at bay.

PAN AMERICAN AIRWAYS SYSTEM
Terminal Building, Customs and Passenger Station, 36th Street Miami, Florida

The firm planned six hangars in a V-shaped configuration in the airport's original design. However, due to the brief life of seaplane service, only two of the hangars were actually constructed. Delano & Aldrich was one of the first architecture firms to treat the airport complex as a cohesive, composed group. A scenic approach flanked by palm trees and grass bisected what was to have been the airport's symmetrical layout. The white stucco, steel-framed terminal was a monumental composition of rectilinear volumes consisting of a two-story center block with one-story wings embellished with glass block, a recessed covered entrance with bronze doors and transom, and a green and gold attic-story frieze of winged globes and rising suns. The terminal's main concourse was also a central, double-height space with clerestory windows and second floor balcony. The interior, however, was highly stylized. Anchored by a ten-foot metal globe rising from a well in the center of floor, the room was decorated with metallic trim, aviation murals, and signs of the zodiac by Barnett Phillips, and dark blue metal windows.[174]

The firm's three Pacific seaplane bases for the airway (1935) were simple and utilitarian. Having discovered that Midway, Wake, and Guam Islands could serve as "stepping stones" across the Pacific, Pan American became the first airline to bridge the ocean with the company's long-range luxurious flying boats. The Midway, Wake, and Guam refueling bases consisted of twelve prefabricated buildings, piers, water tanks, and passenger accommodations constructed out of materials brought over from the United States by steamer. Each hotel contained 24 bedrooms with connecting bathrooms, a dining room, a kitchen, a lobby, and porches.[175]

Delano & Aldrich subsequently won the commission in 1937 for the New York Municipal Airport at North Beach (see pages 174–81), which was renamed LaGuardia Field in 1939. Mayor Fiorella H. LaGuardia hired the firm based on the merit of its design at Dinner Key, a terminal that he had visited and admired.[176] Unrelated to Pan American Airways, the municipal airport was a government-funded project, financed by the City of New York and the Works Progress Administration. It was also considerably bigger than anything Delano & Aldrich had done to date and was, according to Delano, the firm's most important commission.[177] In effect, LaGuardia Field was two airports in one. With both landplanes and seaplanes in operation, Delano and his partner on the project,

PAN AMERICAN AIRWAYS SYSTEM

Terminal Building, Dinner Key
Miami, Florida, c. 1934

Prints and Photographs Division, #303625,
Library of Congress

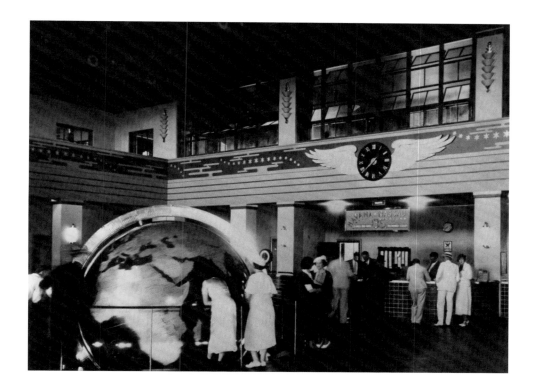

George Licht, designed separate bases for the two modes of travel with corresponding hangars, shops, offices, and passenger accommodations. Runways, aligned with the prevailing winds, were built to the rear of the central landplane terminal and hangars, while the marine terminal with accompanying seaplane harbor, slips, and landing stage was constructed a half-mile away at the edge of Flushing Bay.

Delano & Aldrich continued to develop an airport vernacular of simple massing, materials, and symmetry. All buildings were fireproof, steel-framed structures faced with buff-colored brick and were fluidly composed of rectilinear and cylindrical volumes. The main interior spaces of the terminals were round, double-height, top-lit concourses that, like Dinner Key, were decorated with signs of the zodiac, globes, metallic details, and murals picturing the development of aviation. As was originally intended at Dinner Key, the architects situated the main terminal building at the center of the radiating hangars located on either side. While LaGuardia's architecture and configuration followed that of Dinner Key, Delano & Aldrich incorporated new planning devices into the design. The landplane terminal was capped by a control tower and rotating double-end beacon of 13,500,000 candle power and connected at the rear to a 1,500-foot loading dock where the planes would meet the passengers. Also innovative was the five-sided, heated seaplane hangar with four, forty-foot openings. Its truss structure eliminated the need for columns in the center of the interior and allowed more space for plane storage.

Nobody visualized the industry's phenomenal growth, and soon after its opening in 1940, LaGuardia Field was working at full capacity. Despite Delano's innovative planning solutions, the airport quickly proved to be inadequate. The limitations of the airport site did not allow room for expansion and the firm's rigid plan did not permit flexibility. Therefore, in 1941, the city purchased land along

Jamaica Bay in Idlewild, Queens, with the vision of building an additional municipal airport to accommodate LaGuardia's overflow and the continued growth within the industry. Once again, the mayor asked Delano & Aldrich to prepare drawings for a new airport, this time six times as large as LaGuardia Field.

The new municipal airport, now known as John F. Kennedy Airport, was, according to Delano & Aldrich's plans of 1945, to be built in three stages. It would culminate in a twelve-runway airfield with accommodations for 90 planes and one centralized terminal building. Delano's scheme was based on a dual parallel system—a configuration in which the runways ran in pairs around the terminal building. The first phase of construction, completed in 1948, was temporary. Financed by the sale of Brooklyn's Floyd Bennett Field to the U.S. Navy, the facilities consisted of a long, rectangular terminal, offices, shops, and hangars, and three out of the twelve runways complete.

Unfortunately, the Port Authority, which assumed ownership of the airfield from the insolvent Airport Authority in 1947, lacked the funds to continue building, and air companies, the city, and the architects were in disagreement over the runway configuration and terminal design. As a consequence, Delano & Aldrich's original plan for the airport was never realized. Nonetheless, the firm's enormous, circular terminal with seven 700-foot spokes, or loading platforms, projecting from the building core was an innovation in its own right; its design shifted the hub of the runway system to the actual terminal and loading apron—an unprecedented solution.[178] But however insightful the proposal was, the Port Authority chose to move forward with Wallace Harrison's master plan consisting of decentralized terminals for individual carriers. Idlewild operated with temporary facilities until the mid-1950s.[179]

CONCLUSION

After 1950, Delano & Aldrich's legacy had limited influence on the profession. The subsequent generation was less interested in traditional expression and regarded the firm's work as the last breath of an expiring philosophy.

When the American Institute of Architects awarded William Adams Delano its Gold Medal in 1953, it was the last time the organization honored an American architect working in a classical mode until the end of the twentieth century.[180] Richard Guy Wilson's study on the history of the A.I.A. Gold Medal groups Delano with Paul Cret, Bernard Maybeck, Auguste Perret, Clarence Stein, Louis Sullivan, and John W. Root II—architects who evolved an architecture of "conservative modernism."[181]

That the firm had less influence on American domestic architecture was as much due to the diminishing scale of houses as it was to mass production, which dissipated quality in design and undermined the role of regional and stylistic influences. However, his brilliant airport designs clearly attest to Delano's ability to solve new problems and provided lessons for future architects.

From our perspective, half a century later, we appreciate the firm's positive use of history. They never suffered from "the anxiety of influence," which haunted so many artists in the mid-twentieth century. While out of step with the avant-garde, Delano was never stymied by the modernist movement. For both partners, the practice of architecture was their chance to fuse drawing, painting, and sculpture into an art that they could call their own. Their buildings embody the basic Vitruvian principles, which were the backbone of the Beaux-Arts method: beauty, utility, and fitness. In each design, Delano & Aldrich was able to posit an optimistic position about the presence of the past in the twentieth-century American cultural landscape.

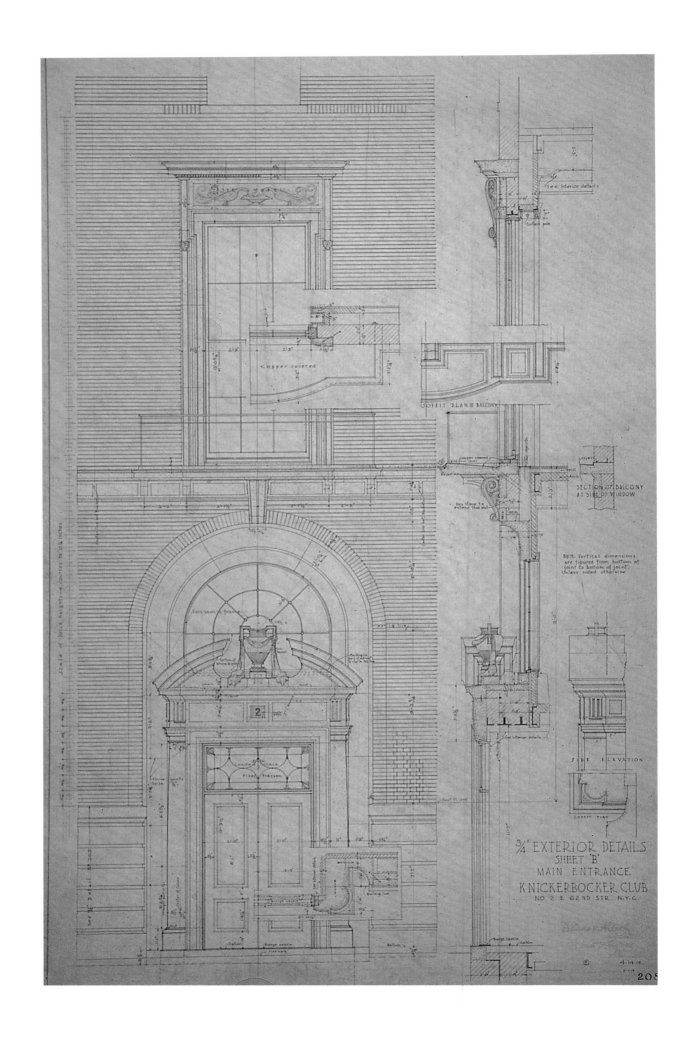

SECTION OF BALCONY
AT SIDE OF WINDOW

NOTE: Vertical dimensions
are figured from bottom of
joint to bottom of joint,
unless noted otherwise

SIDE ELEVATION

¾" EXTERIOR DETAILS
SHEET "B"
MAIN ENTRANCE
KNICKERBOCKER CLUB
NO. 2 E. 62 ND. STR. N.Y.C.

208

TWENTY
DELANO & ALDRICH
PROJECTS

These twenty commissions are presented to demonstrate the skill, style, and range of the Delano & Aldrich practice. In each, regardless of scale, the underlying rigor of Beaux-Arts principles and the poetry of classical language follow as the firm moved from iconic expression to modern classicism. The result of varying conditions, clients, and programs, these projects illustrate the firm's development and form an impressive and fluid body of work.

WALTERS ART GALLERY

Baltimore, Maryland
1904–09

When in 1903, just after the Baltimore fire, Aldrich and I had set up a very modest office in 41st Street, Mr. Walters called me on the telephone one Sunday morning at home and asked if I was building anything in Baltimore. I told him that I was rebuilding a very small hotel that my brother called a saloon. "Well, come down and lunch with me tomorrow," he said, "I'll see if I can improve on that." He told me the sad story of the break between Mr. Morgan and Mr. McKim over the design of the former's library in 36th Street. "Now McKim, I think, is the greatest architect in this country, but he's too damned stubborn. I want to build a gallery in Baltimore for all the treasures my father and I have collected, and I am going to give you boys the chance, provided you do what I tell you." It's easy to imagine with what enthusiasm we set to work. Our plans pleased him and a contract for nearly a million dollars was signed with a contractor. I have often thought it was an outstanding example of faith, hope, and courage, for neither of us had built even a chicken-coop. When the gallery was finished, he was immensely pleased but he said to me, with a twinkle in his cold blue eyes: "I thought McKim was stubborn but you're more so."[1]

After completing his studies in Paris, Delano toured Europe with Arthur Brown, a fellow Beaux-Arts graduate. While they were in Venice, Delano visited Cornelius "Neilly" Vanderbilt III, his friend from Yale, aboard his yacht, *The North Star*. Here, he met Henry Walters, railroad magnate and consummate collector, whose yacht *Narada* was moored alongside Vanderbilt's. Walters was charmed by the young, charismatic architect, and he invited Delano to accompany him on buying sprees at his favorite Venetian antique shops.

With this connection made, Delano & Aldrich was off to an auspicious start; the Walters Art Gallery commission presented an extraordinary opportunity for the fledgling firm. Delano & Aldrich's 28,000 square foot, limestone palazzo designed to house the Walterses' expansive collection was built behind the family's house on Mount Vernon Square. The exterior recalled that of the 1836 Hôtel Pourtalès in Paris designed by architect Félix Duban; the Walterses had visited the building on occasion to see one of France's great private art collections.[2] Like the classical facade of the Hôtel Pourtalès, the Walters Art Gallery had a high, rusticated stone base topped by a string course with a Vitruvian wave. The rather squat, windowless

WALTERS ART GALLERY
Baltimore, Maryland

Rendering of entrance facade

Delano & Aldrich Collection,
Avery Architectural and Fine Arts Library,
Columbia University in the City of New York

second story was divided by paired, fluted Corinthian pilasters supporting a full entablature with a highly carved frieze. It is apparent that Delano had some trouble adapting the French model to his essentially windowless building. While blind windows and a central shield relieved the flat surface of the second story, the overall effect was rather wooden.

The museum's interiors were far more sophisticated than its facades suggested. Delano visited Genoa on his grand tour, soon after meeting Walters, and spent several days studying the town's hillside palaces and Baroque architecture. Inspiration for the gallery's top-lit center court was drawn from the design of Bartolomeo Bianco's open-air courtyard at the Palazzo Balbi in Genoa dating from the 1630s. While the paired marble columns, arcaded loggias, and vaulted spaces directly quoted the Italian prototype, Delano & Aldrich's originality was also discernable. The ground floor stair hall had the gratifying diminutive scale of an outdoor court with rusticated walls, and the sculptural quality of the gallery's main entrance, embellished with a handsome bronze transom, presaged the firm's future work. The overscaled frame of the door slipped into a carved-out concavity within the facade, lending a sculptural depth to the composition. At the rear of the court, a double stair, whose design recalled those of the New York Public Library, led up

Rendering of interior

Delano & Aldrich Collection,
Avery Architectural and Fine Arts Library,
Columbia University in the City of New York

to three top-lit, double-height galleries reminiscent of the grand galleries in nine-teenth-century European palace museums.

As architects, Delano and Aldrich were still learning. When Delano con-sulted with family friend Charles McKim on the gallery's design, McKim ban-tered about the nature of stairs. It was not until after the stair in the entrance vestibule was installed that Delano realized that McKim had been suggesting in an all too elliptical manner that they were too steep. Delano recalled, "Much later, I realized that he had been trying to tell me, without hurting my feelings, that my stairs were far too steep, instead of being, like his stairs, gentle and friendly. So there they are, those brutal stairs of mine, because McKim was kind and I was obtuse."[3] The interior appeared as if it was one bay short, causing the stair to press too close to the front facade. The relationship of the vaulted orders to the front interior wall was unresolved. But despite its shortcomings, the museum was a well-conceived and extraordinary effort for architects just finding their bearings.

The gallery was expanded into a second building, completed in 1974; Delano & Aldrich's original building recently underwent a renovation (1985–88) and con-tinues to house a portion of the Walters Collection.

HIGH LAWN

William B. Osgood Field
Lenox, Massachusetts, 1908–10

By the turn of the twentieth century, Lenox and its surroundings were well established as the "inland Newport," a destination that drew influential New Yorkers, leaders of industry and society.[4] Within the rolling hills of the Berkshires, the wealthy built their "cottages," as they called their expansive summer mansions. William Douglas Sloane, president of W & J Sloane, a furnishings company, commissioned Delano & Aldrich to build a cottage for his daughter, Lila Vanderbilt Sloane, upon her marriage to William B. Osgood Field. The great-granddaughter of Commodore Cornelius Vanderbilt, Lila Sloane Field had grown up summering at her parents' nearby cottage, the vast Elm Court.

An early project, the Fields' 32-room Georgian Revival house exhibited strong Beaux-Arts overtones. The French influence was apparent within and without; French doors, round-headed dormers, and quoins added lightness to the brick design. Bas-relief panels of farm scenes by Mrs. Field's cousin, Gertrude Vanderbilt Whitney, animated the facades, and the High Lawn crest was carved into the limestone above the front entry.

High Lawn's rooms were more elaborately detailed than those in later projects, and were reminiscent of interiors in a Parisian *hôtel particulier*. This was one of the few houses where Delano used full free-standing orders to establish the interior architecture. The monumentality of the main stair hall was created by a full entablature and vaults supported by paired Doric columns. Drawing-room door heads were grandly appointed with broken pediments and urns in relief. The interiors abounded in natural light—even some dressing closets were designed with interior windows or skylights.

The house was carefully integrated into the landscape: gardens, fountains, and pools were aligned with axes extending out from primary rooms. From the garden terrace, one had an unobstructed view over the oversized pool set between *allées* of elms to the hills beyond. Delano cleverly hid the estate's working fields and paddocks below the parterre balustrade so that farm animals did not appear to be grazing on the formal lawn.

Delano showed his brilliant control of the procession through a house and its grounds to exploit the views. The approach was from the west through a thick wood on a drive defined by an *allée* of elms. The entrance court was flanked by small, hipped-roof pavilions, one a playhouse and one a service building. Brick walls sweeping out from the ends of the house to the pavilions embraced the court

HIGH LAWN
Lenox, Massachusetts

BELOW

Garden terrace

Delano & Aldrich Collection,
Avery Architectural and Fine Arts Library,
Columbia University in the City of New York

ABOVE

Tea house and pergola

Delano & Aldrich Collection,
Avery Architectural and Fine Arts Library,
Columbia University in the City of New York

RIGHT

Garden terrace

Delano & Aldrich Collection,
Avery Architectural and Fine Arts Library,
Columbia University in the City of New York

82 ❖

HIGH LAWN
Lenox, Massachusetts

Drawing room

Delano & Aldrich Collection,
Avery Architectural and Fine Arts Library,
Columbia University in the City of New York

and screened the ultimate view. Finally, up the curved entrance steps which seemed to respond to the curved wing walls, one entered into a vaulted hall with a stair at its south end. Passing through the hall directly into the drawing room, the prospect was immediately and dramatically present through massive French doors.

Delano also showed his ingenuity in attaching the kitchen, laundry, and drying yard to the south end of the main body of the house while hiding these elements between the sweep of the south entrance court wall and the brick wall that lined the west side of the garden pergola.

High Lawn continues as a private house and working farm today.

AVALON

Robert S. Brewster
Mount Kisco, New York, 1910

The hilltops of northern Westchester were also a popular area for New York's affluent to build a second or third home. Robert S. Brewster, a college friend of Delano's, built his summer residence, Avalon, above Mount Kisco on property with expansive views and hilly terrain. By this time, the Brewsters were living at 100 East 70th Street, Delano & Aldrich's first large townhouse in New York.

The design of Avalon and its grounds was complicated by the hilly terrain. The house was integrated into the incline of the hill on the property's highest point. The entrance drive crossed over a brook and passed a small, stucco servants' cottage. After crossing the main axis between the house and the south garden, the drive entered an ample court one level below the house where a projecting wing took on the form of an entrance porte cochere. Here, stairs led up to an arcaded outdoor gallery, which extended through the depth of the house to the main entry, round stair hall, and drawing room beyond. The gallery, overlooking a formal rose garden, cleverly masked the service wing that ran behind it.

The drawing room, flanking library, and dining room enjoyed an outlook onto a semicircular grass terrace with *allées* carved into the wooded hills behind. In the foreground were a series of fountains that marked the various radiating axes of the woodland paths leading to the Temple of Love and a charming Palladian-inspired pool house enclosed with cedars. To the south, a sunken, elliptical garden, walled with stone quarried on site, was set below the arrival court and was connected to the house by a path leading down the hill. At a round pergola, the path shifted from the axis to accommodate the eastward slope of the garden.

The Brewsters were more than content with Delano's design. In fact, when Delano's original Avalon burned to the ground, they asked the architect to build a fireproof replica of the house despite Delano's wish to simplify several of the more elaborate details.[5]

The estate has been occupied by a rabbinical college since the late 1940s.

AVALON
Mount Kisco, New York

ABOVE

Drawing room

Delano & Aldrich Collection,
Avery Architectural and Fine Arts Library,
Columbia University in the City of New York

RIGHT

Terrace facade

Delano & Aldrich Collection,
Avery Architectural and Fine Arts Library,
Columbia University in the City of New York

AVALON
Mount Kisco, New York

ABOVE

Pool pavilion

Mattie Edwards Hewitt.
Delano & Aldrich Collection,
Avery Architectural and Fine Arts Library,
Columbia University in the City of New York

OPPOSITE

View from pool pavilion

Mattie Edwards Hewitt. New York State Historical
Association, Cooperstown

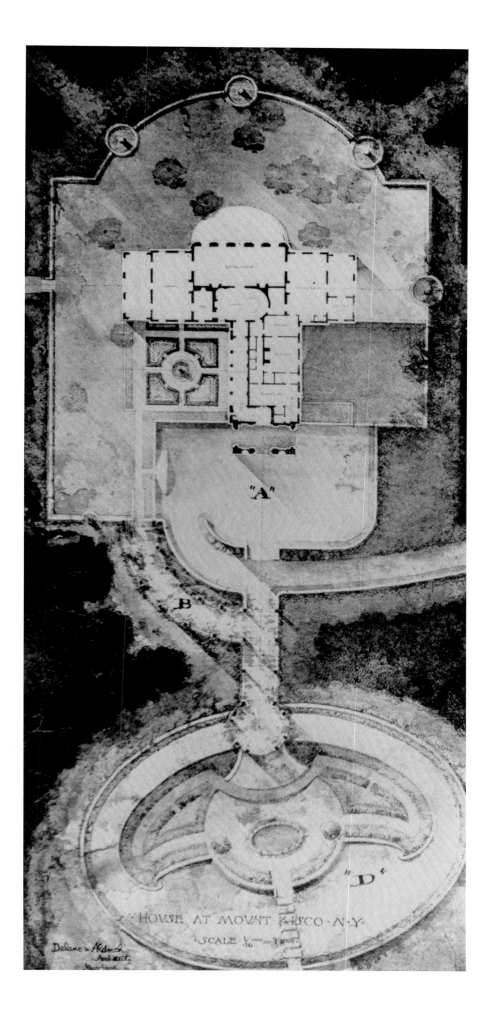

AVALON
Mount Kisco, New York

OPPOSITE

Pergola

Delano & Aldrich Collection,
Avery Architectural and Fine Arts Library,
Columbia University in the City of New York

LEFT

Site plan

Delano & Aldrich Collection,
Avery Architectural and Fine Arts Library,
Columbia University in the City of New York

ARTIST'S STUDIO

Gertrude Vanderbilt Whitney
Westbury, New York, 1913–15

She showed me a bit of woodland she had picked out, well removed from the main house, told me a little of what she wanted, left everything to me, and took a steamer to Europe. It is an architect's dream to have a client who imposes no conditions, but I found this one of the hardest jobs I ever tackled; the plans for the studio and the garden, and the whole question of construction costs, were entirely my responsibility.[6]

For sculptor Gertrude Vanderbilt Whitney, Delano designed a veritable pleasure pavilion tucked away on the Whitneys' extensive estate in Westbury, Long Island. Both an escape and a working artist's space, Mrs. Whitney's studio was furnished with exotic interiors and landscaped with an enclosed formal garden. A rare example of the architect's iconic classical approach, the studio's white stucco facades were crisp and well proportioned, adorned only with a festooned garland frieze at the attic story and punctured by a Palladian-inspired recessed entrance vestibule. The simplicity of its exterior belied the whimsical, eclectic spirit of its interiors, many of which were decorated by Mrs. Whitney's friends and colleagues. Colorful murals and screens by Howard Gardiner Cushing, Robert Winthop Chanler, and Maxfield Parrish seasoned the interiors with an exotic charm.

Stretching the width of the building, the studio had 32-foot ceilings and a large north-facing skylight. French doors opened onto a terrace under a pergola overlooking the private garden with its inlaid, pebble-dash swimming pool, rill, and flower beds where peacocks once strutted about. While the artist completed some of her most important commissions in this studio, the refuge also served as a venue for *vernissages* and parties. The house and its gardens seemed to have an intoxicating affect on visitors. As one guest wrote, "As soon as I saw the strangely dull pool I ran back to the enchanted house and strip and I dove in. Chanler [Robert Winthrop Chanler] came and waiting for him to undress I danced around [the] lawn like a faun in a fine frenzy and frightened [the] queer grey blue silk colored birds who fled awkwardly out of my way."[7]

In the 1980s, architect Charles Meyer added symmetrical kitchen and bedroom wings to the building, transforming it into a house. The studio retains its unique splendor today and is owned by one of Gertrude Vanderbilt Whitney's descendants.

ARTIST'S STUDIO
Westbury, New York

❖ 97

OPPOSITE TOP

Garden façade

Delano & Aldrich Collection, #74893,
Collection of the New-York Historical Society

OPPOSITE BOTTOM

Garden steps

Delano & Aldrich Collection, #74894,
Collection of the New-York Historical Society

LEFT

Site plan by Chester B. Price

Cortissoz, *Portraits of Ten Country Houses*

FOLLOWING PAGES

*Boudoir with murals by
Robert Winthrop Chanler*

Peter A. Juley & Son Collection,
Smithsonian American Art Museum

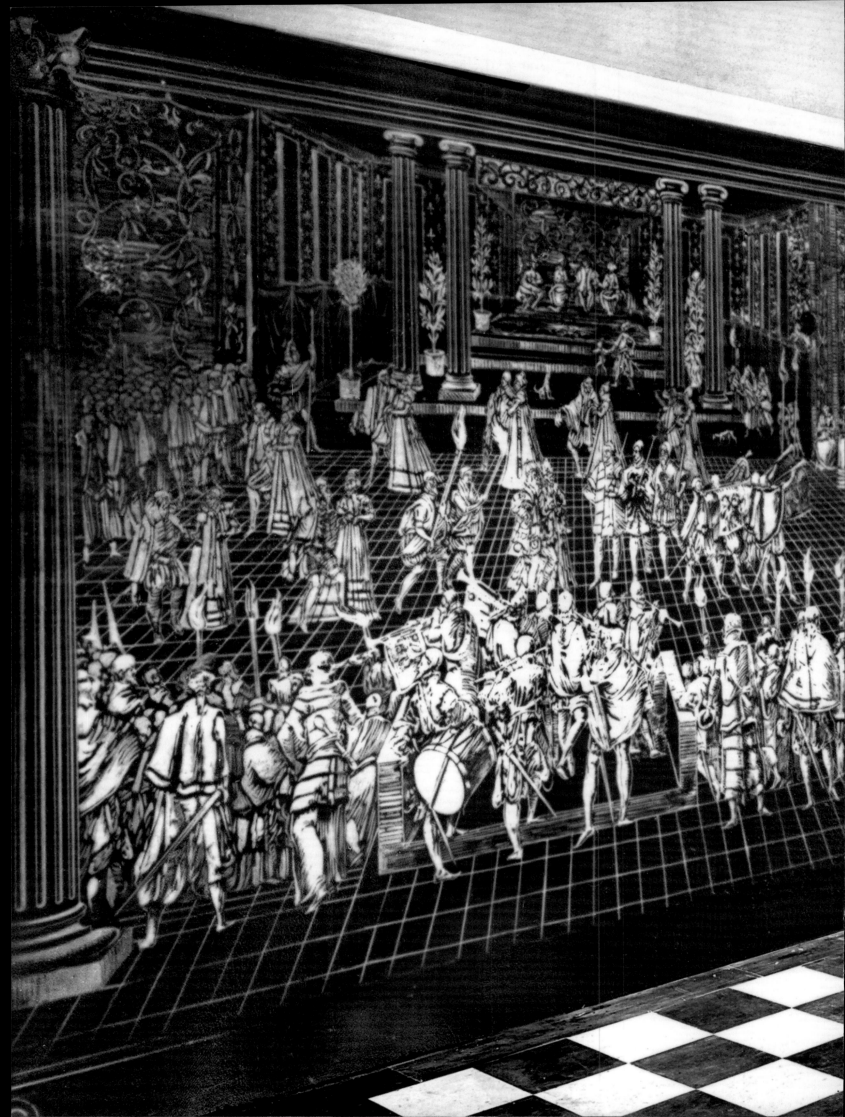

KNICKERBOCKER CLUB

2 East 62nd Street
New York City, 1913–15

In 1912, or thereabouts, the Knickerbocker Club sold its home at 33rd Street and Fifth Avenue and bought the southeast corner of 62nd Street and Fifth Avenue. There were several architect members in the Club and the Building Committee thought it wise, in order to avoid hard feeling, to appoint an outsider. I was the lucky one. It was a big opportunity for a young and unknown architect, for the Club was considered very important in those days. I felt that the elaborate facades of the prevalent French School did not fit in New York and I tried to catch the spirit of my father's house on Washington Square, where I had lived before my marriage. The simple plan and facade I proposed pleased the Committee and everything went along smoothly. The only trouble I had was in convincing the members that it would pay, in light and air, not to build over the southerly part of the property on Fifth Avenue, but instead to build a terrace with wine cellars below.[8]

The Knickerbocker Club, organized in 1871, was formed by members of the Union Club displeased with their club's growing out-of-town membership and relaxed admission standards.[9] By 1913, the club had outgrown its clubhouse on lower Fifth Avenue and the once fashionable neighborhood in which it was located had fallen into decline. In the design of the club's third home at 62nd Street, Delano drew from American, rather than French, precedent; his residentially scaled, Federal Revival clubhouse was inspired by the houses of Washington Square.

The club purchased Princess del Drago's elaborate limestone chateau at the corner of 62nd Street and subsequently added the adjacent parcel. An additional 25 feet along Fifth Avenue enabled Delano to incorporate a private terrace overlooking the park. The carved-out space permitted light and air to filter into the depth of the building. A two-story decorative wall screened the view to the south.

In comparison to the grand palazzo clubhouses from the turn of the century and the Beaux-Arts mansions that once lined Fifth Avenue, Delano's building was notably restrained. Its brick facades, proportions, and eloquent simplicity contributed to the building's quiet impact. Curvilinear balcony grilles and almost Baroque entrance details, atypical of Federal architecture, enlivened the design. Delano's erudite knowledge of tradition enabled him to pull freely from a variety of sources and fuse them successfully into a cohesive, fluid composition.

KNICKERBOCKER CLUB
2 East 62nd Street, New York City

Fifth Avenue elevation

Courtesy of the Knickerbocker Club, New York City

NORTH ELEVATION
KNICKERBOCKER CLVB

62nd Street elevation

Courtesy of the Knickerbocker Club,
New York City

Delano raised the first floor a half story above street level, creating a proper *piano nobile*, a device used frequently in his designs. A double-height entrance vestibule and short stair led to the club's public rooms and a graceful stairwell spiraling up to a top-lit dome with bull's-eye windows.

Delano became a member of the Knickerbocker Club in 1916 once the building was complete; he always considered the clubhouse one of his favorite projects. Its favorable reception among the club's astute membership led to further commissions and catapulted the firm, still relatively unknown at that point, into New York's architectural elite.

The club continues to occupy the building today.

1130 FIFTH AVENUE

Willard D. Straight
New York City, 1913–15

. . . I built for the Straights a house on the corner of Fifth Avenue and 94th Street. After his death, it was bought by Judge Gary and later, from the latter's widow, by Harrison Williams. . . . If I do say so, it's a well planned and lovely house; once inside, it seems much larger than it really is.[10]

Carnegie Hill, by 1913, was a fashionable neighborhood; Andrew Carnegie, who had built his own house on 91st Street at the turn of the century, inspired others to move farther uptown. Delano's house for Willard D. Straight was the northernmost mansion to be built on the avenue. Straight, an editor, diplomat, and financier specializing in Far Eastern relations, originally trained as an architect at Cornell University's College of Architecture. With his wife, Dorothy Whitney Straight, he founded the liberal political journal *The New Republic* and the *Journal of the American Asiatic Association*. Straight's untimely death in 1918 at the age of thirty-eight cut short a brilliant career.

Delano and Straight became close friends after a fortuitous meeting in Havana in 1906, which led to several important commissions for Delano & Aldrich including the renovation of the old Cotton Exchange into India House, a lunch club founded by Straight to promote foreign trade. The firm also designed a country house and stables for the family at Westbury, Willard Straight Hall at Cornell in memory of Straight, and Dartington Hall Nursery School in Devonshire, England, for Straight's widow, Dorothy Straight Elmhirst, a pioneer in progressive education.

Like the Knickerbocker Club, the Straight residence exemplified Delano & Aldrich's delicate yet boldly scaled interpretation of the Federal style. Its elegant and pleasing austerity was achieved through a rigorous composition and straightforward use of materials. Delano's whimsical flourishes, such as the wrought-iron peacock set within the front door fanlight and the Baroque sculpturality of the Wren-inspired attic story bull's-eyes, intermingled seamlessly with the building's refined rectilinear lines. The Adamesque interiors were fitted with Delano & Aldrich's light fixtures. The impressive circular front hall was topped with a dome inset with painted rondels and embellished with niches and a patterned marble floor. Howard Gardiner Cushing's nautical capriccios wrapped the flanking oval dressing rooms.

The Audubon Society and, subsequently, the International Center of Photography occupied the building after the 1950s. Although the exterior is intact, the interiors were gutted as the house was transformed back into a private residence in 2001.

WILLARD D. STRAIGHT HOUSE
1130 Fifth Avenue, New York City

OPPOSITE

Main hall, first floor, view toward dining room

Tebbs and Knell. Delano & Aldrich Collection, Avery Architectural and Fine Arts Library, Columbia University in the City of New York

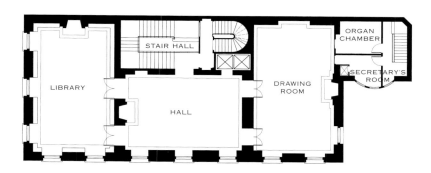

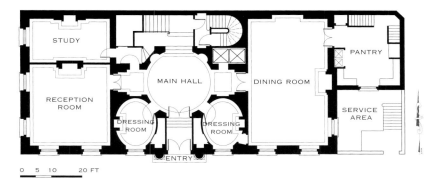

ABOVE

Stair hall

Tebbs Architectural Photo Co. Delano & Aldrich Collection, #74896, Collection of the New-York Historical Society

ABOVE LEFT

First and second floor plans

Drawn by Tiffany Burke from plans in *Architecture* 41 (March 1920): pl. 33

OHEKA

Otto H. Kahn
Cold Spring Harbor, New York, 1914–17

Otto Kahn was a banker, railroad executive, and industrialist as well as a philanthropist and patron of the arts. For Kahn, Delano designed an immense Norman chateau and extensive gardens on a man-made plateau overlooking Long Island Sound. By 1914, when Kahn purchased the property, there was a shortage of available hills with views on the North Shore. Therefore, he simply created his own.

At Oheka, the architects did not rely on the classical orders or elaborate carvings to accentuate the grandeur of the house. Rather, their adroit handling of massing paired with the subtle texturing of stucco with limestone quoins and sills brought life to the facades' crisp lines and grand proportions. To mitigate the overpowering size of the chateau, Delano made the windows appear taller than the cornice line. While maintaining level ceilings on the bedroom floor, the illusion was carried off by false canopies, rendered in lead, on the outside of each window. The roof slates were set in a wavelike pattern, giving the structure weight and depth. Personalizing his work, Delano incorporated wrought-iron linden trees, emblematic of Kahn's hometown in Germany, into the design of the window grilles.

As at Avalon, Delano exploited the topography to enrich the experience of both the landscape and the house and to marry the two. From Oheka's main gate, at a distance, the mansion appeared to hover on the hilltop. The driveway led to a walled entrance circle marked by a tower that served as a hinge to align the final length of the drive with the edge of the south garden. Red cedars planted alongside the drive provided a thick cover that obscured the presence of the house and its gardens. Only after the visitor had passed under the vast entrance arch into the arrival court was the entrance facade revealed.

The design's H-shaped plan allowed Delano to orient the public rooms toward a lawn overlooking the water to the west while service quarters were hidden to the north. The formal, Le Nôtre–inspired gardens abutting the drive were visible only from the south side of the house. Here, Delano's parterres, typically executed in grass, were dominated by pools, generating lively reflective images in the garden. Additional flower gardens were planted below. Kahn's 500-acre estate also included bridle paths, a folly, greenhouses, stables, a gatehouse, tennis courts, and an eighteen-hole golf course. Delano was very proud of the estate's extensive gardens, which also included landscaping by Beatrix Farrand, Olmsted Brothers, and J. J. Levison.

Entrance pavilion

Delano & Aldrich Collection, Avery Architectural and
Fine Arts Library, Columbia University in the City of New York

OHEKA
Cold Spring Harbor, New York

East facade

Delano & Aldrich Collection,
Avery Architectural and Fine Arts Library,
Columbia University in the City of New York

Stable group c. 1924

Previews, Inc. Courtesy of the Society for
the Preservation of Long Island Antiquities,
Cold Spring Harbor, New York

The 72-room mansion was scaled to accommodate Kahn's magnificent lifestyle. Most impressive was the double-height entry hall connecting the arrival court to the main level of the house and terrace, one story higher. The space contained a horseshoe stair inspired by French models, a cross-beamed wooden ceiling, and wrought-iron balustrades worked into the shape of leaf buds and roses. Other grand spaces included the 70-foot by 30-foot ballroom and the 75-foot, concrete-vaulted poolroom, originally intended as the Orangery, which was made accessible from the arrival court by a glassed-in stairwell painted with underwater scenes by Austin Purves.[11]

While Delano delighted in designing Oheka's gardens, he correctly predicted that the estate was too large to survive as a private house. Oheka now functions as a reception venue. From the 1930s to 1970s, the mansion was reincarnated several times, first as Sanita, a retreat for New York City sanitation workers, and later as the Eastern Military Academy.

South facade and garden, 1920

Photo: Mattie Edwards Hewitt. Nassau County Museum Collection, Long Island Studies Institute

OHEKA
Cold Spring Harbor, New York

ABOVE

Garden, 1928

Photo: Mattie Edwards Hewitt. Nassau County
Museum Collection, Long Island Studies Institute

OPPOSITE

Site plan by Chester B. Price

Cortissoz, *Portraits of Ten Country Houses*

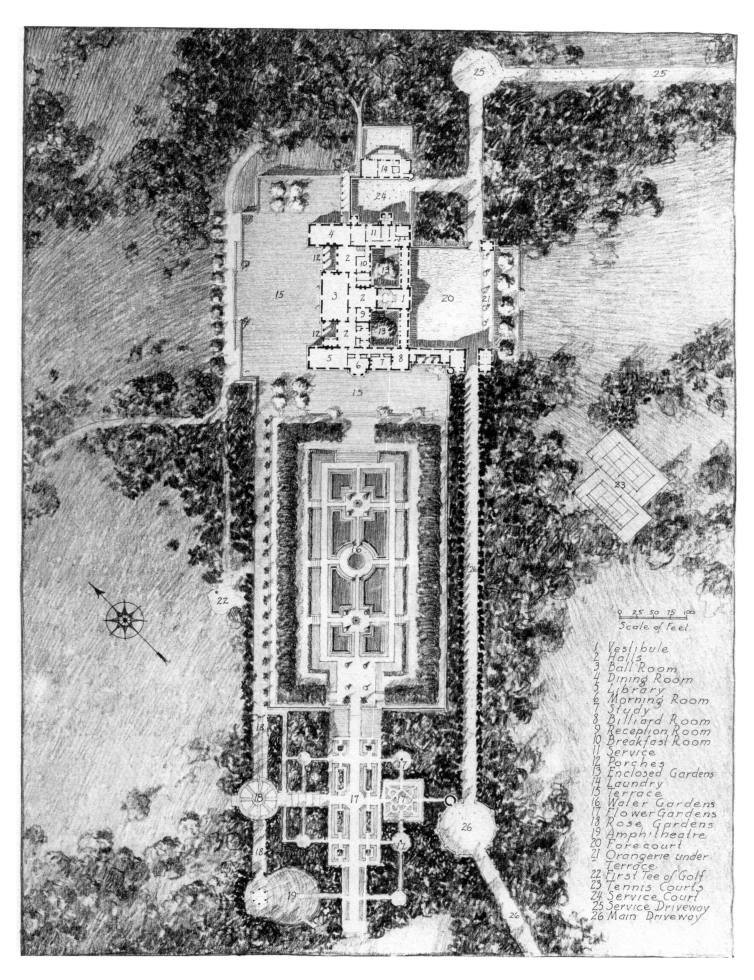

Scale of Feet

1 Vestibule
2 Halls
3 Ball Room
4 Dining Room
5 Library
6 Morning Room
7 Study
8 Billiard Room
9 Reception Room
10 Breakfast Room
11 Service
12 Porches
13 Enclosed Gardens
14 Laundry
15 Terrace
16 Water Gardens
17 Flower Gardens
18 Rose Gardens
19 Amphitheatre
20 Forecourt
21 Orangerie under
   Terrace
22 First Tee of Golf
23 Tennis Courts
24 Service Court
25 Service Driveway
26 Main Driveway

❖ 113

WOODSIDE

James A. Burden, Jr
Syosset, New York, 1916–18

Following closely on the Knickerbocker Club, Mr. and Mrs. James A. Burden asked me to design a house for them at Syosset, Long Island. I planned a large brick house with two wings, which I have always considered one of my best country houses. The rather extensive gardens too gave me great pleasure. It received the Gold Medal of the Architectural League, so you can see others besides myself thought well of it.[12]

The house and grounds that Delano designed for industrialist James A. Burden and his wife, the former Florence Adele Sloane, sister of Lila Sloane Field of High Lawn, received the Gold Medal of Honor from the Architectural League of New York in 1920. Widely published in the architectural press, the Georgian estate was considered by Delano and critics alike as one of the firm's best designs, a house "in which dignity and a gracious friendliness are suavely combined."[13]

The Burdens fancied Southern Colonial architecture, and Annapolis's Whitehall, a 1760s plantation built by Governor Horatio Sharpe, has been considered an inspiration for Woodside. By incorporating elements from the Annapolis house, such as the two flanking, arcaded wings with pavilions and the Flemish bond work into his design, Delano was able to capture the spirit of the Colonial. Yet Woodside was a much larger house that reflected the extensive program required by twentieth-century country estate living; the regularity of its facades and plan were inspired more by Beaux-Arts rationality than Colonial design.[14]

The brick and limestone house was decidedly more restrained than Delano & Aldrich's earlier commissions. The brick veneer stretched tightly across the facade and there was little extraneous detail. The intricate brickwork, balanced proportion of wall to window, arcaded wings punctuated with bull's-eyes, and marble trim added texture to the otherwise spare facades.

In his plan, Delano carefully constructed a sequence where each room evoked a different feeling. An intimately scaled circular hall led to the grand oblong stair hall with rounded ends and, directly across, to a gallery with a south view of the great lawn. Even the openings into the main stair hall, which at first glance were symmetrical, were subtly modeled to exploit the drama of the passage from the front of the house to the back: the arch on the north framed a smaller, trimmed arch with a glazed transom and French doors while the arch on the south, facing the garden, was completely open and made the south gallery spatially continuous with the stair hall.

The house and its dependencies created a compound where the Burdens enjoyed the American equivalent of the elegant life of the British landed gentry— equal measures of refined social ritual and pastoral sports and pleasures. Even a review of Woodside published in 1941 paired pictures of the dining room and Chinese drawing room with views of "Guernseys grazing in front of the house" and "part of the dairy barn."[15] The Prince of Wales stayed at Woodside during his widely publicized vacation on the North Shore of Long Island during the summer of 1924.

Woodside is now a country club; its interiors are somewhat altered.

WOODSIDE
Syosset, New York

ABOVE LEFT
Arcade, c. 1924

Mattie Edwards Hewitt. Nassau County Museum
Collection, Long Island Studies Institute

ABOVE

Entrance, garden facade, c. 1924

Mattie Edwards Hewitt. Nassau County Museum
Collection, Long Island Studies Institute

LEFT

West wing, c. 1924

Mattie Edwards Hewitt. Nassau County Museum
Collection, Long Island Studies Institute

OPPOSITE

Gate and driveway, c. 1924

Mattie Edwards Hewitt. Nassau County Museum
Collection, Long Island Studies Institute

WOODSIDE
Syosset, New York

View from entrance to gate, c. 1924

Mattie Edwards Hewitt. Nassau County
Museum Collection, Long Island Studies Institute

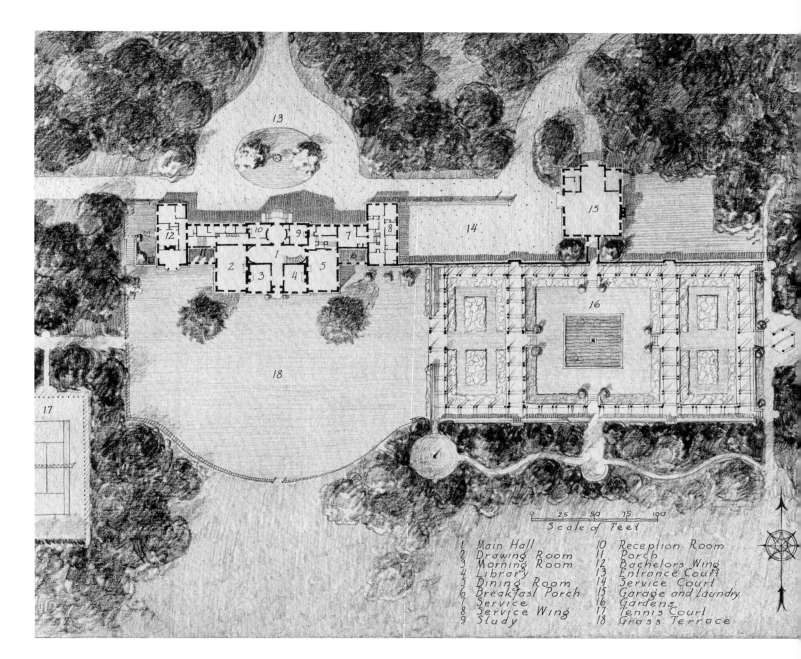

1   Main Hall   10   Reception Room
2   Drawing Room   11   Porch
3   Morning Room   12   Bachelors Wing
4   Library   13   Entrance Court
5   Dining Room   14   Service Court
6   Breakfast Porch   15   Garage and Laundry
7   Service   16   Gardens
8   Service Wing   17   Tennis Court
9   Study   18   Grass Terrace

Site plan by Chester B. Price

Cortissoz, *Portraits of Ten Country Houses*

WOODSIDE
Syosset, New York

TOP

Circular entrance vestibule, c. 1924

Mattie Edwards Hewitt. Nassau County Museum
Collection, Long Island Studies Institute

ABOVE

*The Prince of Wales (bottom left)
descending the front steps of the house,
1924*

Courtesy of Louis Auchincloss

RIGHT

Main hall, c. 1924

Mattie Edwards Hewitt. Nassau County Museum
Collection, Long Island Studies Institute

9 EAST 86TH STREET

William Woodward
New York City, 1916–18

After the Knickerbocker Club, one of the most important houses was the William Woodward House at 9 East 86th Street. It has a really impressive interior, as fitted for the president of a great bank. I imagine it was the Knickerbocker Club that impressed him, for Bill Woodward seldom took chances on anything but horses.[16]

William Woodward, Sr., once president of Hanover National Bank, was an internationally known breeder and racehorse owner. His residence, unlike Delano's other large city houses, was not built on a corner lot; the five-story, limestone and marble mansion, rather, stretched over fifty feet along 86th Street. Given this footprint set between two buildings, Delano handled the space inventively. A one-story entrance pavilion at the western side of the facade created a space for a second floor terrace and upper story loggia. The setback enabled light to enter on two sides of the rooms facing 86th Street, creating bright, airy rooms within, and into the second layer of rooms in the house, which otherwise would have had no light. It also allowed the edifice to stand apart from its neighbors, giving it the appearance, at least from Fifth Avenue, of a freestanding building. With characteristically chaste and restrained facades, Delano created an impressive monument.

The double-height, coffered entry vestibule set the tone of the grandly scaled interiors. A flight of stairs led into the unusually large stair hall with fifteen-foot ceilings and black marble columns. In the Woodward house, circulation was an event and the massive, square stair its pivotal moment. Running to the third floor, the space was top-lit with a lantern suspended from a leaded lay-light, down through the vortex of the stair, to the first floor. The rigorous, straight-edged simplicity of the design amplified the force of the crowning feature under the skylight: portraits of the twelve Caesars framed with anthemia, swags, and oxen heads.

The Town Club of New York, which has occupied the building since 1957, is selling the property as of 2002.

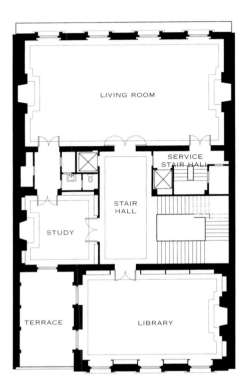

WILLIAM WOODWARD HOUSE
9 East 86th Street, New York City

ABOVE

*Stair hall with portraits
of the twelve Caesars*

John Wallace Gillies. Delano & Aldrich Collection,
Avery Architectural and Fine Arts Library,
Columbia University in the City
of New York

RIGHT

First and second floor plans

Drawn by Tiffany Burke from plans in
Architectural Review 8 [April 1919]: 103

OPPOSITE

Library

John Wallace Gillies. Delano & Aldrich Collection,
Avery Architectural and Fine Arts Library,
Columbia University in the City of New York

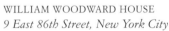

OAK KNOLL

Bertram G. Work
Mill Neck, New York, 1916–18

[Mr. Work] told me very emphatically that he wanted to build a small but perfect house and that it must be built out of income—not one cent of capital! His income must have been large because, when finished the house and gardens had cost nearly a million dollars—a lot for those days . . . . While he lived his friends enjoyed generous and spiritous hospitality in a really beautiful house in the days when architecture meant something more than a machine for living.[17]

Delano always considered his house for Bertram G. Work, president of the Goodrich Rubber Company, one of his best; it embodied all the qualities the firm considered integral to successful country house design. The dignified simplicity of the Palladian design was quietly uplifted by charming details; the house was fitted seamlessly into its surroundings; the gardens were magnificent.

Like Avalon, Oak Knoll sat on a ridge. Sharp drops on three sides of the rise allowed for spectacular views over Oyster Bay and presented complicated contours that Delano exploited to create a complex section of terraces around the house. Defined by a retaining wall, the estate's stone entrance court was adorned with sculpted eagles and wrought-iron "W"s. At the far end, monumental gate posts introduced the steep winding drive which, at the top of the rise, emptied out into a formal, cobbled court, described by Royal Cortissoz in 1924 as "one of the happiest strokes in the architecture of to-day."[18] The stucco house, trimmed with limestone, stretched across its eastern end, hugged by cedars along the lengths of the court; a still pool terminated the western edge. Delano's austere facades were punctuated by a classical portico set into a niche decorated with strap ornament. The house was imbued with Delano's signature lightheartedness: Samuel Yellin's ironwork; balustrades overlaid with dolphins, shells, and turtles; and cornices carved with shells and fish added a whimsical touch. Formal gardens, teahouses, terraces, and pergolas surrounding the house and outbuildings, such as a unique, cottage-style garage with clock tower, were all expertly fitted into the divergent contours of the property.

The classicism of the interiors was adeptly blended with elements that verged on Art Deco. Again, the sea motif prevailed. The amply proportioned rooms were detailed with architect-designed light fixtures, hardware, moldings, and mantels, many of which were also marine-inspired. Gardner Hale's frescos transformed the breakfast room into an orientalist aviary, and the dining room was paneled with wall paintings in the manner of eighteenth-century pastoral scenes. Oak Knoll continues today as a private estate.

OAK KNOLL
Mill Neck, New York

LEFT

South facade

Mattie Edwards Hewitt.
Delano & Aldrich Collection,
Avery Architectural and Fine Arts Library,
Columbia University in the City of New York

TOP

Gate and driveway

Mattie Edwards Hewitt.
Delano & Aldrich Collection,
Avery Architectural and Fine Arts Library,
Columbia University in the City of New York

ABOVE

Garden and tea house, 1920

Mattie Edwards Hewitt. Nassau County Museum
Collection, Long Island Studies Institute

OAK KNOLL
Mill Neck, New York

LEFT

Drawing room, 1920

Mattie Edwards Hewitt. Nassau County Museum
Collection, Long Island Studies Institute

BELOW LEFT

*Morning room with frescos by
Gardner Hale, 1920*

Mattie Edwards Hewitt. Nassau County Museum
Collection, Long Island Studies Institute

BELOW RIGHT

Stair hall, 1920

Mattie Edwards Hewitt. Nassau County Museum
Collection, Long Island Studies Institute

OPPOSITE

Sun room

Mattie Edwards Hewitt.
Delano & Aldrich Collection,
Avery Architectural and Fine Arts Library,
Columbia University in the City of New York

67–75 EAST 93RD STREET

George F. Baker, Jr.
New York City, 1917, 1928, 1931

Although the George F. Baker, Jr., complex was built in several stages, it was a strikingly elegant and cohesive grouping. Construction of the core section of the house, situated on the northwest corner of 93rd Street and Park Avenue, began in 1917 for financier Francis F. Palmer. Executed in the firm's personalized version of Federal and Georgian styles, the austere, brick and marble design was invigorated by a balustraded parapet and a great mansard roof perforated by bull's-eyes, pedimented dormers, and massive chimneys. A quiet, walled garden was situated west of the house, overlooking 93rd Street.

George F. Baker, Jr., who on the death of his father in 1931 inherited the First National City Bank fortune, purchased the Palmer house in 1928 and subsequently added a ballroom wing (1190 Park Avenue) and garage (69 East 93rd Street) in 1928 and a four-story house intended for his father (67 East 93rd Street) in 1931. The complex, when completed, enframed the original Palmer courtyard on 93rd Street; the ballroom, also with frontage on Park Avenue, banded the garden court to the north, the garage and the George F. Baker, Sr., house to the west. While each building had a different character, all shared common classical details, marble trim, and a subtle chain-link belt course at the attic story. The garage wing to the west presented a colossal Ionic colonnade, while the original Palmer house faced east with an elaborately framed window at its midstory stair landing. This inversion of the importance of ornament was a bold and effective stroke, at once providing architectural drama by adding weight to the programmatically less significant garage. Bas-relief panels of cockle and scallop shells were inset above the ballroom and garage windows; the doorway of 67 East 93rd was appointed with a broken pediment inset with sculptural fish. The grandest space in the house was the double-height ballroom decorated with Roman-inspired bas-relief vine moldings, a parquet floor, and massive chandeliers suspended from elaborately molded ceiling rosettes. One reached the ballroom either by the separate Park Avenue entrance or through a rounded vestibule with tulip-crowned capitals in the original building.

The Synod of Bishops of the Russian Orthodox Church Outside of Russia has resided in the original Palmer house and Baker ballroom since 1958; the garage and George F. Baker, Sr., house are privately owned.

GEORGE F. BAKER, JR., HOUSES
67–75 East 93rd Street, New York City

LEFT

Garden facade

John Wallace Gillies. Delano & Aldrich Collection,
Avery Architectural and Fine Arts Library,
Columbia University in the City of New York

RIGHT

Stair hall

John Wallace Gillies. Delano & Aldrich Collection,
Avery Architectural and Fine Arts Library,
Columbia University in the City of New York

Dining room

John Wallace Gillies. Delano & Aldrich Collection,
#58651, Collection of the New-York Historical
Society

60 EAST 68TH STREET

Harold I. Pratt
New York City, 1919–20

I doubt if any house has ever had as much thought and loving care put into it. The Pratts had many beautiful pictures, tapestries and furniture; they asked me to design every architectural detail, including the lighting fixtures. The house has one large paneled room of impressive size— about 40 by 40 feet and nearly 20 feet high—and a library with a gallery on three sides on the same floor.[19]

After returning from the Paris Peace Conference in 1919, Delano designed this seven-story mansion on Park Avenue for the Harold I. Pratt family; Harold Pratt was the youngest son of Charles Pratt, partner of Standard Oil. The dignified, stone-faced residence was stylistically more complicated than its austere facades immediately suggested; both Georgian and Italian undercurrents were at work. While the rusticated base, arched windows, and stone were more Italian in flavor, the rigor of the design and its attenuated lines evoked the design of the Straight house and its Federal and Georgian precedents. The alternating cockle and spiral-shell frieze above the ground floor, the cornice carved with dolphin and shell figures, and the octagonal attic story windows were flourishes that lent the architecture the wit and vitality so distinctive of Delano's work.

After Mr. Pratt's death in 1939, Mrs. Pratt donated the building to the Council on Foreign Relations in memory of her husband. The organization, still at the same address today, added a five story addition (Wyeth & King) in 1954, extending the 68th street facade two bays to the west. In 1946, Mrs. Pratt requested that the architect's name and the building date be carved into the cornerstone; she was concerned that her house would be the only private residence to survive on the avenue. The Pratt house is one of two Delano & Aldrich buildings on which such an inscription appears.[20]

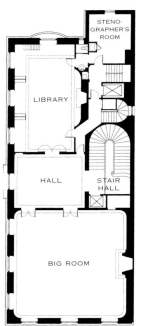

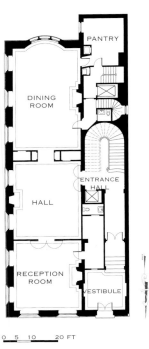

HAROLD I. PRATT HOUSE
60 East 68th Street, New York City

Second floor stair hall

Tebbs Architectural Photo Co.
Delano & Aldrich Collection,
Avery Architectural and Fine Arts Library,
Columbia University in the City of New York

First and second floor plans

Drawn by Tiffany Burke from plans in
Architecture 46 [July 1922]: pl. 108

Drawing room

Tebbs Architectural Photo Co.
Delano & Aldrich Collection,
Avery Architectural and Fine Arts Library,
Columbia University in the City of New York

❖ 139

MIRADOR

Mr. and Mrs. Ronald Tree
Greenwood, Virginia, 1921

ABOVE

Garden facade with arcade

Frances Benjamin Johnston.
Delano & Aldrich Collection,
Avery Architectural and Fine Arts Library,
Columbia University in the City of New York

OPPOSITE

Entrance facade

Frances Benjamin Johnston.
Delano & Aldrich Collection,
Avery Architectural and Fine Arts Library,
Columbia University in the City of New York

Nancy Tree, one of the most attractive women I have ever known, was a dreamer of great dreams, and being bountifully provided with funds by her husband was able to realize them. It was an amusing but rather difficult job for the architect because all her aunts gave advice and warning: Mrs. Dana Gibson said, "You can't touch that front door stoop; that's where Dana courted me." Lady Astor would not let me move or change the old smoke-house for there she had played as a child; this made it difficult to design the garden. And Mrs. Brooks (later the wife of Lord Brand) still felt she had a proprietary interest in the place.[21]

Set in Greenwood Valley against the backdrop of the Blue Ridge Mountains, Mirador—once home to the illustrious Langhorne family—has an evocative history. Colonel James Bowen built Mirador—whose name was inspired by its commanding views—in the 1830s. In the 1890s, Colonel Chiswell Dabney Langhorne purchased the house as a summer retreat for his wife and eight children—the beautiful Irene Gibson (Mrs. Charles Dana Gibson) and Nancy Astor, first female Member of Parliament, among them. The estate passed through the hands of Phyllis Brand, another Langhorne daughter, to Nancy Tree (Lancaster), Langhorne's granddaughter, who acquired the property after her marriage to Ronald Tree, the grandson of Marshall Field, in 1920. Nancy Tree commissioned Delano, a close family friend, to renovate and update the estate, which had gone unchanged for thirty years.

Delano's designs transformed the square, brick, Federal plantation into a grandly appointed house. At Nancy Tree's suggestion, Delano hollowed out the long, narrow main hall, creating an elegant, two-story, top-lit rotunda with a sweeping stair and an inlaid floor compass tied to a central axis. While leaving the front of the house almost untouched, he extended the rear wall of the house fifteen feet on an arcaded base and reiterated its expression in the design of the playhouse pergola and barn group beyond. Delano successfully imported the Blue Ridge Mountains into Mirador's backyard by framing the distant vista with an arched wisteria walk. To the interior, he added Adam-style moldings, imported mantels, paneling, and designed pelmets and fixtures. Mirador was Nancy Tree's first full-scale decorating project; she went on to become a renowned interior decorator.

Delano continued to visit Mirador until the 1950s while the estate was still the center of the extended Langhorne family. Today, the property continues as a private estate.

59–63 WALL STREET

Brown Brothers & Company
New York City, 1927–29

Though Delano & Aldrich was working during the age of rapid skyscraper construction, the firm designed only one New York skyscraper during its fifty-year tenure. Brown Brothers & Company's 37-story tower, set on an irregular lot bounded by Wall, Hanover, and William Streets, was a series of interwoven setbacks. In its design, Delano reconciled the idiosyncrasies of the trapezoidal site with a new building type, producing a coherent and balanced composition. Given the firm's dislike of the skyscraper as a building type, the success of the design was remarkable.

Delano & Aldrich's tower was one of a succession of buildings constructed by Brown Brothers on the same site. The private banking house, founded in 1825, initially moved to 59 Wall Street in 1865. Brown Brothers grew considerably as markets mounted throughout the late nineteenth and early twentieth centuries. The firm was run by a select group of men, many of whom were related to Delano; partners included the architect's father, brother, uncle, and cousins. With this family connection, Delano & Aldrich was in charge of several of the bank's building campaigns; the firm also designed Brown Brothers & Company's Philadelphia office in 1926.

Before the main building commission, Delano & Aldrich designed two consecutive additions to the original 1865 office in 1917 and 1920. Both additions created a separate entrance and offices for partners and visiting clients. In the 1920 scheme, the entrance vestibule was lifted a half level above the street. The vestibule, a rotunda with a coffered ceiling and architect-designed fixtures, featured a curved stair that led to the banking hall and the double-height partners' room paneled in mahogany. Interiors were reminiscent of the architects' clubs uptown and the traditional merchant banks of London.

Delano & Aldrich transported the distinctive ambiance of the small banking hall to Brown Brothers' new offices, completed less than nine years after the opening of their 1920 addition. The skyscraper was designed with two entrances: Brown Brothers retained its 59 Wall Street address on the corner of Wall and Hanover for the partners and clients, while a separate entrance at 63 Wall Street serviced the main elevator banks and tower. The building was accented with fluted piers, stylized spandrels, and colossal medallions representing ancient coins. The interiors easily recalled the firm's previous offices: the elegant entrance rotunda; the grand, double-height banking hall; the intimate, wood-paneled reception spaces; and the imposing partners' room, with a reconstruction of the original 1920 paneling.

The tower rose majestically above Wall Street. The three-sided "light pocket" on Hanover Street generated maximum light within the building. Brickwork spandrels, narrow piers, and limestone accents at the setbacks gave the facades texture and depth; the roofline was accented with oblong bull's-eyes, gargoyles, and a copper hipped roof crested with ironwork.

Brown Brothers moved into the building on May 1, 1929, six months before the stock market crash. In 1930, the bank merged with Harriman Brothers & Company to become Brown Brothers, Harriman & Company; the company occupied the building until 2002.

UNION CLUB

701 Park Avenue
New York City, 1927–33

Much later I was asked to design the Union Club at 69th Street and Park Avenue. This club is much larger than the Knickerbocker and more ornate—more so than I wished—but the Building Committee insisted on a good deal of ornament inside and out, which they were used to in the old club. At the entrance vestibule, it was necessary from my point of view to use a couple of columns, elliptical in plan, in order to meet conditions. I had great difficultly in persuading the members of the Committee that they would never know these columns were elliptical, but they had never seen one (nor had I) so were hard to convince. I had great fun in designing every detail—all the electric light fixtures, mantels, ventilators, etc.[22]

In 1927, Union Club members voted to move from their fifth clubhouse on Fifth Avenue at 51st street. The club decided to purchase land on Park Avenue and 69th Street, despite the fact that many members considered the Upper East Side location too far north to support the club's livelihood. However, having sold their Fifth Avenue building—designed in 1902 by Cass Gilbert and John Du Fais—at the height of the market, they were able to buy land and build a clubhouse three times as large without debt after the crash. The construction of the new building required the demolition of McKim, Mead & White's residence for Geraldyn Redmond and Countess de Laugier Villars (1913–15). Lawrence White, then principal of McKim, Mead & White, asked Delano & Aldrich if they might add the following inscription above the door: "Conceived by the Genius of McKim, Mead and White, Destroyed by the Fury of Delano and Aldrich."[23]

In designing the new Union Club, Delano had to please a committee of members who were devoted to the style of their previous clubhouse, but Delano was able to use the same vocabulary while creating a thoroughly different interpretation of the style. Both buildings were granite, Georgian-inspired designs with muscular rustication and elaborate carving. Delano's stately facades were well suited to the stature and tradition of the Union, New York's oldest men's club.

Several spaces, such as the main hall rotunda and the barrel-vaulted, coffered ceiling by the club's main dining room, referred to areas in the old club. The architects also supervised all decoration, including the wall colors. With air conditioning throughout, "electric-eye" devices to open doors, and three squash courts, the Union was considered superbly modern.[24] Delano inventively incorporated modern

UNION CLUB
701 Park Avenue, New York City

ABOVE

West room detail

Gottscho-Schleisner Collection, #88.1.2.2855,
Museum of the City of New York

OPPOSITE

Entrance rotunda

Gottscho-Schleisner Collection, #88.1.4.1513,
Museum of the City of New York

refinements into the architecture, masking air-conditioning registers throughout the club in ornamental ceiling rosettes and in consoles shaped like ships, peacocks, or backgammon boards, depending on the theme or purpose of the room. In the spirit of the game, the club's original card room was decorated with a stone mantel carved with playing cards and light fixtures and moldings in the shape of the suits. The double-height library was paneled with English oak with a carved frieze on literary themes. The club's tentlike lounge and dressing room, designed by Roman F. Melzer, was exotically decorated with a painted canvas ceiling, fixtures, and wicker furniture. Throughout, Delano's light fixtures, lanterns, and chandeliers were boldly modern. In the most traditional of forums, Delano's spirited brand of classicism emerged vividly; the Union marked a distinct moment in which the firm's work became increasingly distilled and modern.

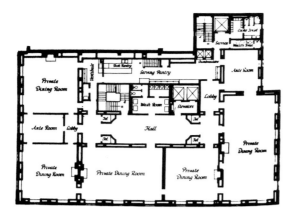

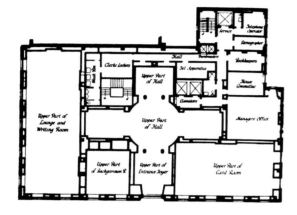

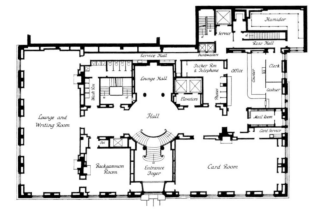

UNION CLUB
701 Park Avenue, New York City

*Plans of first floor, first floor
mezzanine, and second floor*

American Architect 148 [April 1936]: 27. Courtesy of
Avery Architectural and Fine Arts Library, Columbia
University in the City of New York

Library

Gottscho-Schleisner Collection, #88.1.4.1519,
Museum of the City of New York

UNION CLUB
701 Park Avenue, New York City

ABOVE

Governor's dining room, 1935

Samuel H. Gottscho. Prints and Photographs
Division, #303622, Library of Congress

RIGHT

West room, 1935

Samuel H. Gottscho. Prints and Photographs
Division, #303673, Library of Congress

PETERLOON

John J. Emery
Indian Hill, Ohio, 1928–30

A home cannot be built alone
Of bricks and mortar wood or stone
A loving interest must impart
That quality, akin to art
That makes a house a home[25]

Irene and Dana Gibson's daughter, Irene, married John J. Emery in 1926; two years later, the Emerys commissioned Delano to design their Indian Hill mansion. A prominent businessman and philanthropist, John Emery was one of Cincinnati's leading citizens. Educated on the East Coast and abroad, Emery returned to Cincinnati in 1924 where his father and grandfather, Thomas Emery, had laid roots, establishing the Emery name through the family candle company and real estate development firm. As head of Thomas Emery's Sons, Inc., a real estate holdings company developed by his grandfather, father, and uncle, Emery developed the Netherland Plaza and Carew Tower complex designed by Walter W. Ahlschlager and Delano & Aldrich, an innovative mixed-use complex and one of America's Art Deco masterpieces.[26]

Built on the brink of the Depression, Peterloon was one of Delano's last great mansion-scaled houses. Like many of Delano's clients, Emery was a close friend; Delano had worked on Mirador (1921) for the Langhornes and Chelsea (1923–24) for Emery's sister, Alexandra Emery Moore. Peterloon, a restrained Georgian block, was reminiscent of High Lawn and Woodside with its ample brick surfaces and well-proportioned facades. As a later project, Delano's whimsical flourish was more pronounced. Carved snail volutes, scrolling dolphins, and shell-shaped details were integrated into the design. Delano even incorporated a basket of puppies as a motif over the guest wing in tribute to the Emerys' love for animals. Bas-relief panels depicting farm animals by Walker Hancock were inserted above the windows on Peterloon's garden facade.

The 1,200-acre estate had extensive gardens, a farm, and an eight-acre lake. Delano worked with noted Cleveland landscape architect A. D. Taylor to design grounds that consisted of terraces, pools, and gardens.

In 1979, Peterloon was made a foundation and opened to the public.

UNITED STATES POST OFFICE DEPARTMENT BUILDING

Washington, D.C., 1928–35

As Secretary Mellon hoped, we were each given a building to design, and to my lot fell the Circular Plaza on 12th Street and the Post Office Department Building on the west side. The old Post Office today stands like a sore thumb in my Plaza, which is only three-quarters completed because a change of Administration, the Depression, the war with its need for office space … have prevented its removal. This is a sorrow for me for I am sure that this circular plaza would have been handsome; it's one of the disappointments that punctuate the lives of most creators.[27]

For over twenty years, Delano worked on the nation's capital, serving on the National Commission of Fine Arts (1924–28), the Board of Architectural Consultants (1927–33), and the National Capital Park and Planning Commission (1929–46), and as the architectural consultant for the White House (1949–52). The Federal Triangle, an imprint of its Beaux-Arts designers, today stands as the largest unified collection of Beaux-Arts buildings in the world. Delano had an important role in its overall planning and design.

Headed by Charles Moore, the National Commission of Fine Arts was an advisory body responsible for overseeing the city's architectural development. In 1926, Delano and his colleagues on the committee outlined guidelines for the ongoing Triangle project in keeping with the formalized composition envisioned by Pierre Charles L'Enfant (1791) and the subsequent McMillan Plan (1901). In 1927, Andrew Mellon invited Delano to join the Board of Architectural Consultants, a group composed of seven architects charged with the actual planning and designing of the Triangle. Each of the board members—Edward Bennett (president), Louis Ayres, Arthur Brown, Milton B. Medary, John Russell Pope, Louis Simon, and Delano—was allotted one building in the Triangle group to design. The commission approved the various designs as they developed and made sure they worked with one another successfully. Because Delano served simultaneously on both committees, he acted as both architect and adviser in the design process and a link between the two interrelated bodies.

The buildings of Louis Ayres (Department of Commerce), Arthur Brown (Interstate Commerce Commission), and Delano formed the western section of the ensemble and were intended to enclose an open green mall. As the pivot of the western and eastern portions of the Triangle, the centerpiece of the design was to have been Delano's circular plaza based loosely on Mansart's Place Vendôme.

UNITED STATES POST OFFICE
DEPARTMENT BUILDING
Washington D.C.

ABOVE

Lobby

Commercial Photo Co., Washington
Delano & Aldrich Collection,
Avery Architectural and Fine Arts Library,
Columbia University in the City of New York

ABOVE RIGHT

Interior courtyard

Commercial Photo Co., Washington.
Delano & Aldrich Collection,
Avery Architectural and Fine Arts Library,
Columbia University in the City of New York

OPPOSITE

Arcade

Theodor Horydczak. Prints and Photographs
Division, #303641, Library of Congress

Willoughby J. Edbrooke's Romanesque Post Office, however, was never removed from the site, as was originally planned. With Franklin D. Roosevelt's presidency (1933–45), governmental priorities shifted away from Washington's building campaign, and Delano's plaza was never realized in its entirety.

Although the monumental limestone buildings were broken up by myriad open courts and arched driveways, much like the Louvre-Tuileries complex, they moved seamlessly into one another, differentiated by subtle variations in classical language. Delano's United States Post Office Department Building, bordered by Pennsylvania Avenue, was distinguished by Ionic columns, tympanums with allegorical sculpture pertaining to the mail system, lanterns, and carved eagle door heads. Delano's end pavilions with their rusticated bases, arches, paired Ionic columns, and balustraded mansard roofs with dormers referred directly to classical Parisian models. His interiors were characteristically restrained: the orders were simplified to abstraction, and details and ironwork were stylized. In the design of the building, the allied arts were strongly represented—the commission urged collaboration among the arts. Public spaces were richly decorated with work by such WPA artists as Reginald Marsh, Chaim Gross, and Louis Slobodkin. Under the supervision of Adolph A. Weinman, a group of young artists including Walter Hancock, Sidney Waugh, George H. Snowden, Joseph E. Renier, Frederick G. R. Roth, and Anthony de Francisci designed and executed the decorative sculpture throughout the building.[28] Delano's two seven-story, marble spiral stairs were dramatically lit by chandeliers composed of globes and signs of the zodiac; staircase balusters were embellished with cast bronze serpents, emblematic of Mercury, the messenger of the gods.

According to one critic of the Triangle Group, the "gilded vulgarity" of the buildings exemplified all that was "artificial and false" in society and the United States Post Office Department Building was "a battery of columns" so complex that one would need a diagram to figure it out.[29] However, in its design, Delano "rejoice[d] in the elimination of unnecessary detail, the invention of new ornament to replace many that [were] shopworn, and for the delightful use of newly invented materials."[30] Despite the building's traditional guise, its facades were sparse in detail and its interiors were more Art Deco than Beaux-Arts. Delano incorporated a discreet "curtain wall" into his design of the interior courtyards to light the seven-story stairwells that looked out onto the enclosed spaces.

AMERICAN GOVERNMENT BUILDING

Place de la Concorde
Paris, France, 1929–32

. . . I have been trying to bring what the United States Government wants in its new building on the Place de la Concorde into harmony with what the city guards as one of its most precious assets—the beauty of the Place de la Concorde.[31]

In the mid-eighteenth century, royal architect Jacques-Ange Gabriel designed the Place de Louis XV, Paris's original imperial square, which is now known as the Place de la Concorde. His design was safeguarded by governmental ordinances, which regulated all subsequent construction on the square. Grimod de la Reynière, a wealthy landowner, built his mansion in 1769, completing the tetrad of buildings along the square's northern edge. This *hôtel*, however, never conformed to the architectural standards of Gabriel's designs—the Ministry of the Navy, the Hôtel Crillon, and the Hôtel Talleyrand.

In 1928, the United States government purchased the *hôtel*, then occupied by an artists' association, and Andrew W. Mellon, secretary of the Treasury, selected Delano & Aldrich as architects for the American Government Building, which was to replace the building on the site. As an American, Delano was especially honored to design a public building on one of Paris's most sacred spots—this would have been beyond his wildest dreams when studying at the Ecole des Beaux-Arts, yet the experience proved grueling. The firm was at the hands of three reigning bodies— the U.S. government, the architect of the *arrondissement*, and the Architecte Voyer of the City of Paris, all of whose agreement and approval were needed to bring the plan into effect.

With Victor Laloux, who led Delano's atelier at the Beaux-Arts, as consulting architect, Delano & Aldrich executed a building that fit seamlessly into the historic square while maintaining its modern identity. In its design, Delano essentially created an updated version of what Gabriel might have envisioned for the northwest side of the square. The building was a modern facility with an underground parking garage, which housed under one roof the chancellery, consulate, and twelve commissions working in France. Its design was based roughly on the Hôtel Talleyrand (also known as the Hôtel Saint Florentin), the corresponding building at the northeast corner. Story heights, rooflines, and window patterns were carried through. Its design was also linked to that of the Hôtel Crillon and the Ministry of the Navy—the axis of their grand arcade extended through Delano's forecourt, ter-

AMERICAN GOVERNMENT BUILDING
Place de la Concorde, Paris, France

Entrance facade and Hôtel Crillon

Delano & Aldrich Collection,
Avery Architectural and Fine Arts Library,
Columbia University in the City of New York

Main hall

Delano & Aldrich Collection,
Avery Architectural and Fine Arts Library,
Columbia University in the City of New York

FOLLOWING PAGES

Gates

Delano & Aldrich Collection, #74897,
Collection of the New-York Historical Society

minating in a fountain set within an emulative arch. Restrained in design, the stone building, capped in lead-coated copper, was unobtrusively decorated with U.S. seals and sculpted eagles by Paul Jennewein.

The interiors were American in spirit; rooms were decorated with early American furniture, and the mechanics, elevators, flooring, and tiles were imported from the United States. From the carved cornices of interweaving "U. S. A."s in the Wallace Library and Protocol office to the architect's whimsical lanterns, the Delano touch was evident throughout. The characteristic mix of iconic and abstract classicism prevailed: columns with capitals of shells and scrolling serpents supported the ceiling of the coffered main hall. In plan, the building was tightly organized around an open court; the ambassador's chambers occupied the center rooms of the building overlooking the Place de la Concorde.

The building continues as the American embassy and chancery.

STERLING DIVINITY SCHOOL

Yale University
New Haven, Connecticut, 1930–32

Delano designed seven buildings for his alma mater; the Divinity School quadrangle, located a half mile from the downtown Yale campus, was his final and most ambitious project at the university. Steeped in tradition, the Divinity School, founded in 1822, had long been considered the preeminent course of study for those entering the Protestant ministry. Delano's campus was the school's third home at Yale.

Like Jefferson's design for the University of Virginia, Delano's campus was a self-contained academic village on a hill. The Divinity School plan, consisting of a series of arcaded, two-story, brick pavilions, revolved around a focal point: Marquand Chapel. The campus was originally designed for a flat site at the head of Hillhouse Avenue and had consisted of a quadrangle enclosed by buildings with the chapel marking its front entrance. The sloping site on which the school was eventually built provided grounds for a more ingenious architectural solution. Delano's campus was broken into three distinct, yet fluid, spaces for residential, learning, and communal purposes. Two octagonal guest pavilions, marking the entrance to the school, and six arcaded pavilions, which originally housed 160 students, looked up at the Wren-inspired chapel at the crest of the hill. Through the play of site levels, Delano stressed the importance of the chapel within the plan, emphasizing its severe lines and verticality in relation to the small-scaled pavilions. He skillfully wrapped the composition around the back of the chapel, creating secondary greens to the rear of the building. By expanding the campus behind the chapel, Delano masked the size of large common areas, such as the dining room and gymnasium, by integrating their bulk into the downhill slope directly behind the quadrangle.

The severity of Delano's brick facades was relieved by white trim on the pavilion fronts and a lofty steeple adorned with swags and sculptural eagles. As with Delano's clubs and houses, interiors were detailed with stylized light fixtures and shell moldings. The chapel with its apsidal chancel recalled the ordered ambiance of the New England meeting house, yet a new level of sophistication was introduced into the simple rectangular space with Delano's glass and chrome-plated brass chandeliers with gold-plated eagles and tassels.

Currently, the campus is undergoing an extensive renovation by R. M. Kliment & Frances Halsband Architects; it will continue as the Divinity School.

STERLING DIVINITY SCHOOL
Yale University, New Haven, Connecticut

Dining hall

Yale Alumni Weekly. Photographs of Sterling Divinity Quadrangle, Yale University [RU 628]. Manuscripts and Archives, Yale University Library

Model

Photographs of Sterling Divinity Quadrangle, Yale University [RU 628]. Manuscripts and Archives, Yale University Library

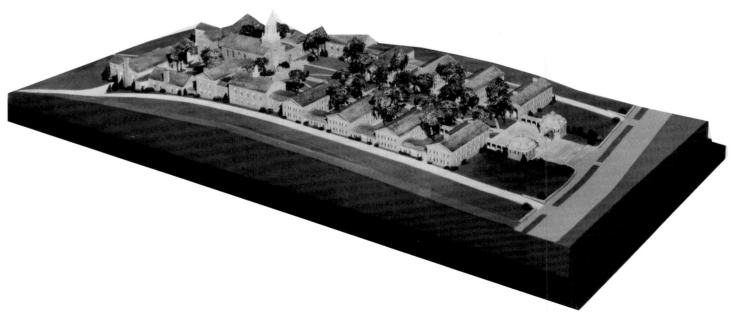

Interior of Marquand Chapel

Yale Alumni Weekly. Photographs of Sterling
Divinity Quadrangle, Yale University [RU 628].
Manuscripts and Archives, Yale University Library

NEW YORK MUNICIPAL AIRPORT

LaGuardia Field
Flushing, New York, 1937–42

The airport, now named LaGuardia Field, was violently attacked by the opponents of the City and Federal governments: "Far too big—a waste of money." It did not take long to discover that it was much too small and was soon over-crowded, as it is today. We designed two administration buildings and seven enormous hangars. When it opened, I gave a dinner to a hundred or more of my friends in the restaurant run by the Hotel New Yorker, overlooking the field. It rained all day and I feared my party would be a failure, but by the dinner hour it cleared and a beautiful crescent moon rode in a blue sky. The runways were filled by arriving and departing planes, and the planes were stationed on the apron below the restaurant. Flying was comparatively new in those days and my guests were thrilled, as I was, by the sight.[32]

Although Delano never actually flew, he was thrilled by aviation. The New York Municipal Airport commission presented the architect, in the twilight of his career, with an exciting challenge. Mayor Fiorello H. LaGuardia initiated the project, cosponsored by the Works Progress Administration under Franklin D. Roosevelt and the City of New York, as part of an extensive transportation campaign to improve the city as it emerged from the Depression. The new airport, which replaced New York's inadequate Floyd Bennett Field in Brooklyn, provided the city with jobs and vied for supremacy with Newark, New Jersey's 1928 airport which was, at that point, the only major facility that conveniently serviced the metropolitan area. When LaGuardia Field was completed, it was considered the largest and most modern airport in the country; it was dedicated on October 15, 1939—in time for the 1939 World's Fair—and was fully operational by 1940.

The 201-acre site chosen for the airport overlooking Flushing Bay, combined with 357 additional acres of infill, created a large, unobstructed area. While the openness of the site enabled the airport to be built to order, Delano and his partner, George Licht, were faced with the new questions posed by the novel concepts associated with air travel.

The field was intended as a link for passengers traveling overseas and within the United States. The clipper ships for transoceanic travel were much larger than landplanes and required a different type of infrastructure. At LaGuardia Field, Delano and Licht designed separate landplane and seaplane bases with accompa-

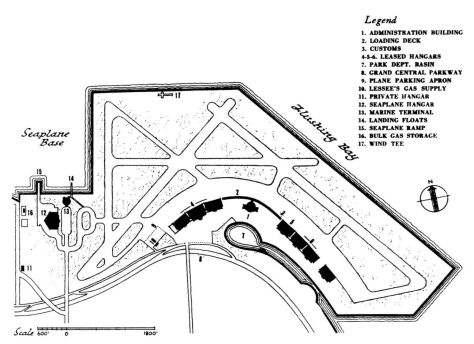

Seaplane Base

Flushing Bay

Scale 600' 0   1800'

NEW YORK MUNICIPAL AIRPORT
LaGuardia Field, Flushing, New York

ABOVE

Landplane terminal building

W. Hoff. Delano & Aldrich Collection,
Avery Architectural and Fine Arts Library,
Columbia University in the City of New York

RIGHT

*View from landplane terminal with
"Spirit of Flight" by T. A. and I. W. Beck*

Delano & Aldrich Collection,
Avery Architectural and Fine Arts Library,
Columbia University in the City of New York

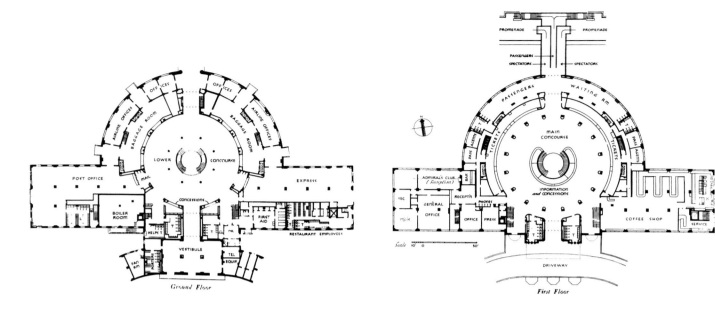

NEW YORK MUNICIPAL AIRPORT
LaGuardia Field, Flushing, New York

Plan, landplane terminal

Pencil Points 21 [October 1940]: 622. Courtesy
of Avery Architectural and Fine Arts Library,
Columbia University in the City of New York

nying hangars, offices, and shops for the two types of craft in operation. Essentially, it was two airports in one; the marine terminal, at the edge of Flushing Bay, was a half mile away from the centrally located landplane terminal. As was originally intended at Dinner Key, Miami, three hangars flanked the main terminal building on either side, disposed in a curve. All buildings were fireproof, steel-framed structures faced with buff-colored brick.

At LaGuardia, Delano & Aldrich continued to develop an airport vernacular of simple massing, materials, and symmetry. Both of airport's terminal buildings were fluidly composed of rectilinear and cylindrical volumes in which the main interior spaces were round, double-height, top-lit concourses—the "rotunda," used frequently in Delano & Aldrich's houses and clubs, here was ascribed a new use. The two-story landplane terminal was a spare and symmetrical design enhanced by panels of stylized classical elements in black brick and a great steel eagle by T. A. and I. W. Beck surmounting the building. The main concourse was a sleek, modern space decorated by Arthur Covey with gold zodiac signs set within the dome and a huge globe suspended from the skylight. Simplified, black marble columns with stainless-steel trim, pink-gray marble floors, cast-aluminum light fixtures, and tall, glass-brick windows offset Covey's bold decorations. Circumscribed by ticket offices, the concourse led to two offshooting wings that contained restaurants and offices; the second floor included a restaurant and terrace overlooking the fields.

Functions within the terminal's plan were clearly demarcated, facilitating an easy flow of people through interior and exterior spaces. Arriving and departing passengers were allocated to separate levels in the main terminal building, a planning device that is still used in major airports today.[33] Departing passengers entered

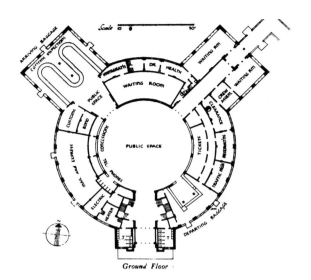

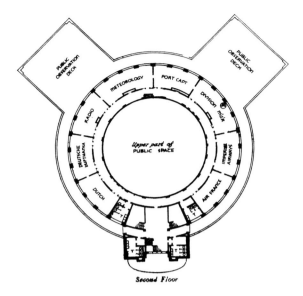

Plan, marine air terminal

Pencil Points 21 [October 1940]: 630. Courtesy of
Avery Architectural and Fine Arts Library,
Columbia University in the City of New York

on the upper level of the building via a ramp; they passed through the central concourse and ticket area to the waiting room with connections out to a 1,500-foot steel
and glass loading platform. The platform extended against the rear of the landplane
terminal along the arcing line between the two sets of hangars and was connected
to the concourse by a bridge. Described by John Walter Wood, early airport critic,
as "an important innovation" and "the airport's most striking feature," the platform
enabled 24 planes to be loaded and unloaded simultaneously.[34] Eleven small, heated dispatcher booths were spaced the length of the platform; boarding and deplan-
ing passengers moved through the lower level of the platform while airport visitors
watched from the upper deck.[35] The apron, radiating out from the loading dock,
connected to taxi runways, which, in turn, connected to the four, 400-foot-wide
runways—the longest being 6,000 feet—designed in accordance with the relative
wind speed and frequency—or "wind rose."

The marine air terminal was distinguished by a stylized frieze of gold dolphins
against blue waves circumscribing the building. While Delano used this motif
repeatedly in his designs—such as at Oak Knoll, Peterloon and The Brook, its
occurrence here was most fitting. Inside, the circular concourse was dramatically
enhanced by James Brook's mural "Flight," depicting flying in its various stages of
development. The continuous, twelve-foot-high painting was set against dark green
marble walls and gray marble floors. Brooks's mural, covered over in the 1950s, was
restored in 1980. The landplane terminal and loading platform were demolished in
the early 1960s to make way for Harrison & Abramovitz's new terminal—three
times as large—with four arms extending out from the rear of the building. The
marine air terminal was designated a New York City landmark in 1980 and continues to serve the airport.

FOLLOWING PAGES

*Concourse in landplane terminal
decorated by Arthur Covey*

Gordon Hamilton. Delano & Aldrich Collection,
Avery Architectural and Fine Arts Library,
Columbia University in the City of New York

CHRONOLOGY
AND CATALOGUE RAISONNÉ

The Delano & Aldrich Collection at Avery Library, Columbia University in the City of New York, contains partial, undated lists of the firm's work. Our Catalogue Raisonné has been constructed around these lists with input from books, historical societies, building owners, descendants of the original owners, and the firm's drawings.

Buildings have been ordered chronologically by the year in which the project was begun, if known. We have attempted to attribute the project to either Delano (D) or Aldrich (A) when possible and to name its current status. If extant, the building's function is specified only if it has changed from its original purpose. If the building's status is not listed, it is unknown. Houses listed as estates are larger properties that include Delano & Aldrich-designed outbuildings and/or gardens.

Delano retired from the firm in 1949 and assumed the role of advisory partner on January 1, 1950. Also in the early 1950s, several partners—H. S. Waterbury, George A. Licht, and Herbert Godwin—retired or died. The firm continued under the name "Delano & Aldrich" until the mid 1950s under Alexander McIlvaine, Mrs. Delano's nephew.

1871

Chester Holmes Aldrich born on June 1, 1871, in Providence, Rhode Island.

1874

William Adams Delano born on January 21, 1874, in New York, New York.

1891

Delano graduates from The Lawrenceville School.

1893

Aldrich graduates from Columbia University with a Bachelor of Philosophy degree.

1895

Delano graduates from Yale University with a Bachelor of Arts degree.

1898

The two men meet at Carrère & Hastings while working on competition entries for the New York Public Library.

1900

Aldrich receives diploma from the Ecole des Beaux-Arts.

1902

Delano receives diploma from the Ecole des Beaux-Arts.

1903

Delano and Aldrich form partnership.

Aldrich awarded honorary doctor's degree by Columbia University.

Delano becomes professor of design, Columbia University (1903–10).

EGERTON L. WINTHROP, JR., ESTATE, Muttontown Meadows, Muttontown Road, Syosset, New York; 1903–4; (D); extant: Nassau Hall, Nassau County's Muttontown Preserve.

ANSON PHELPS STOKES HOUSE, addition, Elm Street, New Haven, Connecticut; (D); extant: Yale Faculty Club.

JOHN D. ROCKEFELLER ESTATE, Kykuit, Pocantico Hills, New York; (A); 1903–8; extant: altered 1910, museum.

1904

V. EVERITT MACY HOUSE, Hathaway, Onteora, New York; (A).

ROBERT PRUYN HOUSE, gate lodge, Camp Santanoni, Newcomb, New York; 1904–5; (D); extant: State Forest Preserve.

WALTERS ART GALLERY, North Charles Street, Baltimore, Maryland; 1904–9; (D); extant.

PHILADELPHIA ORPHANAGE, South Providence Road, Wallingford, Pennsylvania; 1904–5; extant: Wallingford Convalescent, Rehabilitation, and Nursing Center.

JOHN E. PARSONS HOUSE, Lounsbury, library wing, Boston Post Road, Rye, New York; c. 1904; extant.

ST. CLOUD PRESBYTERIAN CHURCH, pastor's manse, Prospect Avenue, West Orange, New Jersey; (D); extant.

1905

BEAUX-ARTS CASINO, with Maurice Prevot, Huntington, New York; 1905–7; demolished: 1950s.

JUDGE LEARNED HAND HOUSE, White Acre, Mclain Street, Mount Kisco, New York; (A); 1905-06; extant.

CHRISTIAN HERTER ESTATE, El Mirasol, Micheltorena Street, Santa Barbara, California; (A); demolished: 1969.

1906

JUDGE LEARNED HAND HOUSE, interior alterations, 142 East 65th Street, New York City.

WILLIAM SLOANE ESTATE, Merestead, Byram Lake Road, Bedford, New York; 1906–7; (D); extant.

JOHN WILLIAM DAVIS HOUSE, Mattapan, alterations, Overlook Road, Lattingtown, New York; c. 1906; extant.

1907

ROBERT BREWSTER HOUSE, 100 East 70th Street, New York City; 1907–8; (D); demolished: 1948.

J. F. HAVEMEYER HOUSE, Hancock Place, Ardsley–on–Hudson, New York; (A); extant.

925 PARK AVENUE, New York City; 1907–9; extant.

PALMERTON HOSPITAL; Palmerton, Pennsylvania; 1907–8; demolished.

FRANKLIN FURNACE HOSPITAL, Franklin Furnace, Pennsylvania; c. 1907.

1908

Delano awarded a Bachelor of Fine Arts by Yale. Listed at Yale as a "Degree Conferred in Course."

CHARLES E. MERRILL HOUSE, Hidden Way, alterations, Bay Avenue, Huntington; 1908 and 1923; (A).

W. B. OSGOOD FIELD ESTATE, High Lawn, Lenox, Massachusetts; 1908–10; (D); extant.

FRANKLIN ROOT HOUSE, Northern Avenue, Bronxville, New York; extant.

HENRY BARBEY BUILDING; 15–17 West 38th Street, New York City; 1908–9; (D); extant: offices.

1909

WILLIAM ADAMS DELANO HOUSE, alterations, 131 East 36th Street, New York City; (D); extant.

G. SCHIRMER BUILDING, 3–7 East 43rd Street, New York City; (D); extant: Berkeley College's New York City campus.

RUSSELL SAGE MUSIC SCHOOL, "Olivia Hall," Northfield, Massachusetts; extant: Northfield–Mount Hermon School.

FORSYTH WICKES ESTATE, Gray Crag, Tuxedo Park, New York; extant: altered.

NEW HAVEN LAWN CLUB, alterations and additions, Whitney Avenue, New Haven, Connecticut; 1909–10; destroyed in fire (1929) and redesigned by Douglas Orr.

1910

HOWARD GARDINER CUSHING HOUSE, 121 East 70th Street, New York City; extant.

BRONSON WINTHROP ESTATE, Jericho–Oyster Bay Road, Muttontown, New York; c. 1910; (D); demolished: 1980.

WILLIAM ADAMS DELANO ESTATE, Muttontown Corners, Syosset–Brookville Road, Muttontown, New York, 1910–11; (D); extant.

ROBERT ABERCROMBIE LOVETT ESTATE, Green Arbors, alterations to Carrère & Hastings house, Sheep Lane, Lattingtown, New York; c. 1910; demolished: 1938.

FRANCIS LEBARON ROBBINS, JR., STUDIO, Ben Robyn, West Mall Drive, West Hills, New York; c. 1910; extant.

MISS E. A. WATSON HOUSE, Sherman Avenue, Gedney Farm, White Plains, New York; c. 1910; extant.

ROBERT S. BREWSTER ESTATE, Avalon, Pines Bridge Road, Mount Kisco, New York; (D); extant: Yeshiva Farm Settlement School.

ROLLIN SALTUS ESTATE, Norwood, South Bedford Road, Mount Kisco, New York; c. 1910; extant.

WILLIAM GIBSON BORLAND ESTATE, Mount Kisco, New York.

HAROLD I. PRATT HOUSE, Welwyn, alterations to Babb, Cook & Willard house, tennis court building, Crescent Beach Road, Glen Cove; extant: Welwyn Preserve, Holocaust Memorial and Education Center of Nassau County.

JESUP MEMORIAL LIBRARY, 34 Mount Desert Street, Bar Harbor, Maine; 1910–11; (D); extant.

WILLIAM DOUGLAS SLOANE ESTATE, Elm Court, interior alterations, Lenox, Massachusetts; extant.

DR. H. D. LLOYD HOUSE, Newtonville, Massachusetts, c. 1910.

WILLIAM WOODWARD HOUSE, The Cloister, alterations, Marine Avenue, Newport, Rhode Island; c. 1910; demolished.

E. G. STODDARD HOUSE, East Rock Road, New Haven, Connecticut; c. 1910; extant: Albertus Magnus College.

HENRY SABIN CHASE HOUSE, alterations, Church Street, Waterbury, Connecticut; demolished.

ETHEL KETCHAM HOUSE, Thornhenge Road, Bellport, New York; extant.

Thorne Estate: Delano & Aldrich Collection, Avery Architectural and Fine Arts Library, Columbia University in the City of New York

W. V. S. THORNE ESTATE, Gateways, Normandy Heights Road, Morristown, New Jersey; 1910–11; extant: Morristown Unitarian Fellowship.

THATCHER M. BROWN ESTATE, Ballymena, Red Bank, New Jersey; c. 1910; extant.

ST. CLOUD PRESBYTERIAN CHURCH, Sunday School building, Prospect Avenue, West Orange, New Jersey; (D); extant: altered.

NEW YORK ORTHOPAEDIC DISPENSARY AND HOSPITAL, main building and nurses' home, Mamaroneck Avenue, White Plains, New York; c. 1910; demolished: c. 1990.

1911

MISS MARION HAGUE HOUSE, 161 East 70th Street, New York City; 1911–12; extant.

Alexander Estate: Mattie Edwards Hewitt. Delano & Aldrich Collection, Avery Architectural and Fine Arts Library, Columbia University in the City of New York

MRS. C. B. ALEXANDER ESTATE, Chapin Road, Bernardsville, New Jersey; (A); extant.

WALTER L. GOODWIN HOUSE, Hartford, Connecticut; (A).

WRIGHT MEMORIAL HALL, Yale University, Elm Street, New Haven, Connecticut; 1911–12; (D); extant.

DAY MISSION LIBRARY, Yale University, New Haven, Connecticut; (D); demolished: 1931.

Root House: Delano & Aldrich Collection, Avery Architectural and Fine Arts Library, Columbia University in the City of New York

FRANKLIN ROOT HOUSE, Plateau Circle West, Bronxville, New York; 1911–15; extant.

KING GEORGE V INSTITUTE BUILDING, International Grenfell Foundation, St. John's, Newfoundland, Canada; (D); extant.

EMILY CALDWELL HOUSE, Highfield, alterations and addition, Lake Road, Dublin, New Hampshire; extant.

1912

ALLEN WARDWELL HOUSE, 127 East 80th Street, New York City; extant.

WILLARD STRAIGHT ESTATE, Applegreen, alterations, Wheatley Road, Old Westbury, New York; 1912–13; (D); demolished: c. 1970.

L. K. THORNE HOUSE, Babylon, New York.

HENRY HEWITT HOUSE, sleeping porch addition, No. E Street, Tacoma, Washington.

1913

KNICKERBOCKER CLUB, 2 East 62nd Street, New York City; 1913–15; (D); extant.

WILLARD D. STRAIGHT HOUSE, 1130 Fifth Avenue, New York City; 1913–15; (D); extant: interior alterations.

MARSHALL J. DODGE HOUSE, facade alterations, 37 East 68th Street, New York City; extant.

Donnelly & Ricci Studio: Delano & Aldrich Collection, Avery Architectural and Fine Arts Library, Columbia University in the City of New York

DONNELLY & RICCI STUDIO, 335 East 46th Street, New York City; demolished: 1960s.

GERTRUDE VANDERBILT WHITNEY STUDIO, Wheatley Road, Westbury, New York; 1913–15; (D); extant with additions by Charles Meyer.

MRS. MARGARET CHANLER ALDRICH ESTATE, Rokeby, facade alteration; potting shed and renovation of greenhouse into garage and chauffeur's apartment, Barrytown-on-Hudson, New York; c. 1913; (A); extant.

DOROTHEA HOUSE, John Street, Princeton, New Jersey; c. 1913; extant: Dorothea van Dyke McLane Association.

1914

Colony Club Ballroom: *Architecture* 33 [April 1916]: pl. 70. Courtesy of Avery Architectural and Fine Arts Library, Columbia University in the City of New York

COLONY CLUB, 564 Park Avenue, New York City; 1914–16; (A); extant.

India House: Mattie Edwards Hewitt. Delano & Aldrich Collection, Avery Architectural and Fine Arts Library, Columbia University in the City of New York

INDIA HOUSE, alterations, One Hanover Square, New York City; 1914 and 1924; (D); extant: Bayard's restaurant.

FLOWER HOSPITAL, private patients' pavilion and Warner annex, upper Fifth Avenue, New York City; c. 1914; demolished.

LEWIS CASS LEDYARD, JR., HOUSE, Westwood, pool and tennis court building, Berry Hill Road, Oyster Bay Cove, New York; extant: Orthodox Church in America.

OTTO H. KAHN ESTATE, Oheka, West Gate Drive, Cold Spring Harbor, New York; 1914–17; (D); extant: reception venue.

Wortham Estate: Delano & Aldrich Collection, Avery Architectural and Fine Arts Library, Columbia University in the City of New York

JAMES WORTHAM ESTATE, Normandie, Ocean Avenue, Newport, Rhode Island; (D); extant.

WILLIAM WOODWARD HOUSE, Belair, alterations and addition to c. 1745 building, Tulip Grove Drive, Bowie, Maryland; extant: museum, Belair Mansion and Stud Farm.

HOPE FARM SCHOOL AND CHAPEL, Verbank, New York; 1914 and 1924; (A): extant: Fountains at Millbrook (retirement community).

MISS ELIZABETH R. HOOKER HOUSE, Edgehill Road, New Haven, Connecticut: extant.

INTERNATIONAL GARDEN CLUB, alterations and conservatory additions to the Bartow-Pell Mansion, Shore Road, Bronx, New York; extant: museum.

1915

St. Bernard's School: Courtesy of the St. Bernard's School, New York City

ST. BERNARD'S SCHOOL, 4 East 98th Street, New York City; extant with additions.

MABEL I. BARNES HOUSE, facade alteration, 67 East 91st Street, New York City; extant.

VICTOR MORAWETZ ESTATE, Three Ponds, South Woods Road, Woodbury, New York; (D); extant: Oyster Bay Golf Course.

MALCOLM McBURNEY ESTATE, East Islip, New York; c. 1915; extant.

GEORGE WHITNEY ESTATE, Bacon Road, Old Westbury, New York; c. 1915; extant.

GERTRUDE VANDERBILT WHITNEY HOUSE, Whitney Cottage, ballroom addition, Bellevue Avenue, Newport, Rhode Island; demolished.

ALEXANDER CHAPEL, Clinton Farms, New Jersey; extant: chapel at Edna Mahan Correctional Facility for Women.

1916

WILLIAM WOODWARD HOUSE, 9 East 86th Street, New York City; 1916–18; (D); extant: Town Club of New York.

WILLARD D. STRAIGHT GARAGE, 162 East 92nd Street, New York City; extant.

GREENWICH SETTLEMENT HOUSE, 29 Barrow Street, New York City; 1916–17; (A); extant.

DELANO & ALDRICH OFFICE, 126 East 38th Street, New York City; (D); extant: office.

BERTRAM G. WORK ESTATE, Oak Knoll, Cleft Road, Mill Neck, New York; 1916–18; (D); extant.

JAMES A. BURDEN ESTATE, Woodside, Muttontown Road, Syosset, New York; 1916–18; (D); extant: Woodcrest Country Club.

LEONOR F. LOREE ESTATE, Bowood, Mount Pleasant and Prospect Avenues, West Orange, New Jersey; demolished.

FREDERIC A. DELANO HOUSE, Algonac, alterations, Newburgh, New York; (A).

CHRIST CHURCH, parish house, Church Street, Hartford, Connecticut; 1916–17; extant.

1917

Aldrich takes leave of absence from firm to serve as director general of civil affairs for the American Red Cross commission to Italy (1917–19).

FRANCIS PALMER HOUSE, 75 East 93rd Street, New York City; 1917–18; (D); extant: Russian Orthodox Church Outside Russia.

JAMES H. LANCASHIRE HOUSE, interior alterations and rear addition, 7 East 75th Street, New York City; extant.

WILLIAM SLOANE HOUSE, 686 Park Avenue, New York City; 1917–19; (D); extant: Italian Cultural Institute.

GIFFORD PINCHOT HOUSE, Grey Towers, alterations, Grey Towers Drive, Milford, Pennsylvania; (A); extant: museum.

GRAND CENTRAL ART GALLERIES, Grand Central Terminal Museum, New York City; demolished.

BROWN BROTHERS & COMPANY, addition, 59 Wall Street, New York City; demolished: 1927

1918

Delano serves as assistant to Joseph E. Grew, secretary of the United States delegation to the Peace Conference in Paris (1918–19).

MISSES PARSONS ESTATE, Stoneover, Lenox, Massachusetts; c. 1918; demolished: 1950s.

YALE UNIVERSITY PRESS, ALTERATIONS, Yale University, Elm Street, New Haven; extant: university office building.

ANNEX TO THE PRINCE GEORGE HOTEL, 14 East 28th Street, New York City; c. 1918.

1919

HAROLD I. PRATT HOUSE, 60 East 68th Street, New York City; 1919–20; (D); extant: Council on Foreign Relations.

R. FULTON CUTTING HOUSES, 12, 14, and 16 East 89th Street, New York City; 1919–22; (D); extant: Saint David's School.

MRS. ALFRED G. VANDERBILT ESTATE, Holmwood, Lenox, Massachusetts; c. 1919; extant: Foxhollow Resort, altered.

CUSHING MEMORIAL ART GALLERY, Bellevue Avenue, Newport, Rhode Island; 1919–20; (D); extant.

MAX BOHM STUDIO, Summit Avenue. Bronxville, New York; extant.

1920

Watriss Estate: Cortissoz, *Portraits of Ten Country Houses*

FREDERIC WATRISS ESTATE, Valentine's Lane, Old Brookville, New York.

R. FULTON CUTTING, JR., HOUSE, 15 East 88th Street, New York City; 1920–22; (D); extant.

Griscom Estate: Cortissoz, *Portraits of Ten Country Houses*

LLOYD GRISCOM ESTATE, Huntover, East Norwich–Oyster Bay Road, Muttontown, New York; (D); demolished: c. 1980.

SAMUEL L. FULLER AND CHARLES L. TIFFANY APARTMENTS, 43 Park Avenue, New York City; (A); demolished.

BROWN BROTHERS & COMPANY, ADDITION, 59 Wall Street, New York City; demolished: 1927.

MRS. LYDIG HOYT HOUSE, Mulberry Corner, alterations to 1735 house, Woodbury, New York; c. 1920.

EDWIN FISH ESTATE, Airdrie, Chicken Valley Road, Matinecock, New York; (D); extant.

PAYSON McL. MERRILL ESTATE, Woodmere, New York; (A).

HUGH KNOWLTON ESTATE, Muttontown Road, Muttontown, New York; c. 1920s; extant.

BURROUGHS WELLCOME LABORATORY BUILDING, Scarsdale Road, Tuckahoe, New York; c. 1920s.

RODNEY CHASE HOUSE, Thomaston Road, Watertown, Connecticut; c. 1920s; extant.

1921

EDNA BARGER HOUSE, alterations, 145 East 61st Street, New York City.

MRS. RONALD TREE ESTATE, Mirador, alterations to an 1820s house, Greenwood Road, Greenwood, Virginia; (D); extant.

ROBERT P. PERKINS ESTATE, Huntington, Long Island; (A).

STERLING CHEMISTRY LABORATORY, Yale University, Prospect Street, New Haven, Connecticut; 1921–23; (D); extant.

VALERIA HOME, with Charles H. Higgins, Oscawana, Cortlandt, New York; 1921–37; extant: developed with condominiums.

GIFFORD PINCHOT HOUSE, alterations, Rhode Island Avenue, Washington, D.C.; demolished.

1922

THIRD CHURCH OF CHRIST SCIENTIST, 583 Park Avenue, New York City; 1922–24; (D); extant.

Astor Estate: Mattie Edwards Hewitt. Nassau County Museum Collection, Long Island Studies Institute

VINCENT ASTOR ESTATE, Cloverley Manor, West Shore Road, Sands Point, New York; extant.

ROBERT G. MCGANN ESTATE, Fairlawn, East Deerpath, Lake Forest, Illinois; 1922–23; extant.

Round Hill Club: Courtesy of the Round Hill Club, Greenwich, Connecticut

ROUND HILL CLUB, Round Hill Road, Greenwich, Connecticut; 1922–24; (D); extant.

SAGE HALL OF FORESTRY, Yale University, Prospect Street, New Haven, Connecticut; 1922–24; (D); extant.

FIRST PRESBYTERIAN CHURCH OF BENSON-HURST, church and community building, West 10th Street & Q Avenue, Brooklyn, New York; 1922–23, 1928–29.

EUGENE FIELD MEMORIAL, Lincoln Park, Chicago, Illinois; extant.

Chapin Estate: Tebbs and Knell. Delano & Aldrich Collection, Avery Architectural and Fine Arts Library, Columbia University in the City of New York

CHARLES M. CHAPIN ESTATE, Elsoma, Pine Tree Boulevard (originally Thomasville/Tallahassee Road), Thomasville, Georgia; 1922–23; (A); extant.

ALUMNI STUDY, Foundation House, The Lawrenceville School, Lawrenceville, New Jersey; (D); extant.

PALACE FOR ARCHBISHOP E. P. ROCHE, St. John's, Newfoundland, Canada; 1922–24; extant: Episcopal Library.

TWILLINGATE HOSPITAL, Twillingate, Newfoundland, Canada; 1922–24; extant: Notre Dame Bay Memorial Hospital.

655 PARK AVENUE, New York City; never built.

1923

ELBRIDGE STRATTON HOUSE, facade alteration, 11 East 61st Street, New York City; extant: Lubin House of Syracuse University.

ARTHUR DUEL HOUSE, interior alterations, 4 East 65th Street, New York City.

HENRY G. GRAY HOUSE, facade alteration, 134 East 71st Street, New York City; extant.

SAGE, ANDREW G. C., alterations, New York City; c. 1923.

1040 PARK AVENUE, New York City; 1923–24; extant.

J. HENRY LANCASHIRE HOUSE, 11 East 69th Street, New York City; 1923–24; extant.

Babcock Estate: Robert W. Tebbs. Delano & Aldrich Collection, Avery Architectural and Fine Arts Library, Columbia University in the City of New York

RICHARD F. BABCOCK ESTATE, Hark Away, Woodbury Road, Woodbury, New York; c. 1923; demolished: 2000.

BENJAMIN MOORE ESTATE, Chelsea, Northern Boulevard, Muttontown, New York; 1923–24; service wing added 1929; (D); extant: Muttontown Preserve.

STATEN ISLAND SAVINGS BANK, Water and Beach Streets, Stapleton, Staten Island, New York; 1923–24; (A); extant.

BRONX RIVER PARKWAY COMMISSION, bridges at Scarsdale (bridge 28) and Tuckahoe, New York; 1923–24; extant.

SMITH COLLEGE MUSIC SCHOOL (SAGE HALL), Northampton, Massachusetts; 1923–26; (A); extant.

SACRED HEART CONVENT MUSIC BUILDING (PIUS X HALL, SCHOOL OF LITURGICAL MUSIC), 425 West 130th Street, New York City; 1923–24; extant: part of John H. Finley Public School 129.

WILLARD STRAIGHT HALL, Cornell University Union, Ithaca, New York; 1923–25; (D); extant.

TUDOR & STUART CLUB LIBRARY, Gilman Hall, Johns Hopkins University, Baltimore, Maryland; 1923–25; extant.

1924

Delano serves as member of the National Commission of Fine Arts (1924–28).

MRS. CHARLES P. HOWLAND HOUSE, facade alteration, 107 East 64th Street, New York City; extant.

A. GORDON NORRIE HOUSE, interior alterations, 153 East 61st Street, New York City.

THE BROOK, 111 East 54th Street, New York City; 1924–25; (D); extant.

RODERICK TOWER ESTATE, Northern Boulevard (off), Brookville, Old Westbury, New York; extant: New York Institute of Technology.

ROBERT W. FOWLER ESTATE, Happy Valley Farm, Katonah, New York; (A).

HOPE FARM LIBRARY, Verbank, New York; (A); Fountains at Millbrook.

DUTCH REFORMED CHURCH, Wheatley and Brookville Roads, Brookville, New York; (D); extant.

MRS. WILLIAM ASTOR CHANLER HOUSE, addition, 700 Acres Island, Isleboro, Maine; (D); extant.

CONDÉ NAST APARTMENT, 1040 Park Avenue, New York; extant: divided into smaller apartments.

ALUMNI WAR MEMORIAL BUILDING, The Lawrenceville School, Lawrenceville, New Jersey; (D); demolished.

1925

J. J. HEWITT HOUSE, with Sutton, Whitney & Dugan Associates, No. D Street, Tacoma, Washington; 1925–26.

JOHN DENNISTON LYON ESTATE, Duck Point Road, Matinecock, New York; c. 1925; extant.

MRS. GEORGE W. FOLSOM ESTATE, Sunnyridge, Lenox, Massachusetts; 1925–26; extant.

BLISS MAUSOLEUM, Woodlawn, New York; (A).

Harkness Hall: Delano & Aldrich Collection, Avery Architectural and Fine Arts Library, Columbia University in the City of New York

WILLIAM L. HARKNESS HALL, Yale University, Wall Street, New Haven, Connecticut; 1925–26; (D); extant.

MECHANICS AND METALS NATIONAL BANK, Harlem Branch, New York City; c. 1925.

WILLIAM H. BUSK ESTATE, Branch Brook House, Lincoln Avenue, Purchase, New York; c. 1925.

WILLIAM H. WHEELOCK ESTATE, Rye, New York.

Fathers' Building: Courtesy of The Lawrenceville School, Lawrenceville, New Jersey

FATHERS' BUILDING, The Lawrenceville School, Lawrenceville, New Jersey; (D): extant.

WESTFIELD TRUST COMPANY, Westfield, New Jersey; 1925–27.

Hammond Estate: Mattie Edwards Hewitt. Courtesy of the Society for the Preservation of Long Island Antiquities, Cold Spring Harbor, New York

1926

PAUL HAMMOND ESTATE, Muttontown Lodge, East Norwich–Oyster Bay Road, Syosset, New York; (D); extant.

J. C. CLARK ESTATE, Ripplebrook, Far Hills, New Jersey.

GERTRUDE ELY HOUSE, Wyndham Barn, alterations to eighteenth–century barn, Bryn Mawr, Pennsylvania; demolished: 2001.

BROWN BROTHERS & COMPANY, Walnut Street, Philadelphia, Pennsylvania; 1926–27; extant.

NORRIE GATES, Rhinebeck, New York; extant.

STATEN ISLAND HOSPITAL, private patients' pavilion and nurses' home, Tompkinsville, Staten Island, New York; extant.

1927

Delano serves on the Board of Architectural Consultants, Treasury Department, Washington, D.C. (1927–33).

Wood Estate: Howell, *Noted Long Island Homes*. Courtesy of the Society for the Preservation of Long Island Antiquity, Cold Spring Harbor, New York

CHALMERS WOOD ESTATE, Little Ipswich, South Woods Road, Syosset, New York; 1927–28; (D); demolished.

BROWN BROTHERS & COMPANY, 59–63 Wall Street, New York City; 1927–29; Lunch Club; (D); extant: offices.

UNION CLUB, 701 Park Avenue, New York City; 1927–33; (D); extant.

MISS CHAPIN'S SCHOOL, 100 East End Avenue, New York City; 1927–28; (A); extant with additions.

THOMAS M. DEBEVOISE ESTATE, Hidden Springs Farm, Village Road, Green Village, New Jersey; (D); extant.

DWIGHT W. MORROW HOUSE, Deacon Brown's Point, North Haven, Maine; (A); extant.

H. RIVINGTON PYNE ESTATE, Shale, Bunn Road, Bedminster, New Jersey; extant.

Payson Estate: Howell, *Noted Long Island Homes*. Courtesy of the Society for the Preservation of Long Island Antiquities, Cold Spring Harbor, New York

CHARLES S. PAYSON ESTATE, Greentree, Shelter Rock Road, Manhasset, New York; 1927–1928; (D); extant: North Shore Unitarian Universalist Society.

Williams Estate: Howell, *Noted Long Island Homes*. Courtesy of the Society for the Preservation of Long Island Antiquities, Cold Spring Harbor, New York

HARRISON WILLIAMS ESTATE, Oak Point, alterations to Babb, Cook & Willard house, tennis court, and pool building, Bayville Avenue, Bayville, New York; 1927–28; (D); demolished: 1960s, extant: tennis court building.

Dater House: Mattie Edwards Hewitt. Delano & Aldrich Collection, Avery Architectural and Fine Arts Library, Columbia University in the City of New York

ALFRED W. DATER HOUSE, Altair, Fisher's Island, New York; c. 1927; extant.

HUBERT E. ROGERS ESTATE, The Crossways, Scarborough Road, Scarborough, New York; 1927–29; extant.

MRS. JUSTINE B. WARD HOUSE AND CHAPEL, Mora Vocis, North Mountain Drive, Ardsley–on–Hudson, New York; extant: Ardsley Country Club.

FRANK MUHLFELD ESTATE, Englewood, New Jersey; c. 1927; extant.

AUGUSTUS WADSWORTH HOUSE, Suitsme Farm, Manchester, Vermont; extant.

S. FORRY LAUCKS ESTATE, York, Pennsylvania; 1927–28, addition: 1942; (D).

FIRST LUTHERAN CHURCH, parish house, Western Avenue, Albany, New York; 1927–29; extant.

THE WHITE HOUSE, Washington D.C.; alterations to third floor and new roof; (D); extant.

1928

Lewis Library: Delano & Aldrich Collection, Avery Architectural and Fine Arts Library, Columbia University in the City of New York

WILMARTH S. LEWIS HOUSE, library addition, Main Street, Farmington, Connecticut; 1928–29; extant: Lewis Walpole Library, Yale University.

GEORGE F. BAKER, JR., HOUSE, ballroom addition to Palmer house and garage, 1190 Park Avenue and 69 East 93rd Street; New York City; (D); extant: ballroom—Russian Orthodox Church Outside Russia, garage private.

GREENWICH SETTLEMENT HOUSE, Arts and Crafts Building, 16 Jones Street, New York City; (A); extant.

AMERICAN RED CROSS BUILDING, Old Country Road, Mineola, New York; demolished: 2002.

HARRY C. CUSHING ESTATE, Muttontown Road (off), Muttontown, New York; extant.

DWIGHT W. MORROW ESTATE, Next Day Hill, Next Day Hill Drive, Englewood, New Jersey; 1928–31; (A); extant: the Elizabeth Morrow School.

CHARLES M. CHAPIN ESTATE, Dunleith, Chapin Road, Bernardsville, New Jersey; 1928–29; (A); destroyed in fire: 1961.

J. LESTER PARSONS ESTATE, Broadacre, and swimming–pool building, Llewellyn Park, West Orange, New Jersey; 1928–1929; extant.

CHARLES EDISON ESTATE, Landmoore, Lynwood Way, Llewellyn Park, West Orange, New Jersey; 1928–30; extant.

JOHN J. EMERY ESTATE, Peterloon, Hopewell Road, Indian Hill, Ohio; 1928–30; (D); extant: Peterloon Foundation.

PAN AMERICAN AIRWAYS SYSTEM, terminal building, customs and passenger station, 36th Street, Miami, Florida; demolished.

UNITED STATES POST OFFICE DEPARTMENT BUILDING, 12th and Pennsylvania Avenue, Washington, D.C.; 1928–35; (D); extant: Ariel Rios Building.

WESTMINSTER PRESBYTERIAN CHURCH, alterations, Chestnut Street, Albany; New York; 1928–30; extant.

KINNAN GATEWAY, The Lawrenceville School, Lawrenceville, New Jersey; (D); extant.

GEORGE W. GARDNER HOUSE, Brooklyn, New York; c. 1928.

1929

Delano serves as member of the National Capital Park and Planning Commission (1929–46).

E. LAWRENCE JONES ESTATE, Drake Road, Cincinnati, Ohio; extant.

Nightingale–Bamford School: Courtesy of the Nightingale–Bamford School, New York City

NIGHTINGALE–BAMFORD SCHOOL, 20 East 92nd Street, New York City; extant with additions.

AMERICAN RED CROSS CHAPTER HOUSE, 315 Lexington Avenue, New York City; (A); extant: Permanent Mission of Cuba to the United States.

GREENWICH SETTLEMENT HOUSE MUSIC SCHOOL, 46 Barrow Street, New York City; (A); extant.

PRENTISS L. COONLEY ESTATE, Folly Farm, Division Street, Great Barrington, Massachusetts; 1929–31; extant: American Institute of Economic Research.

WILLIAM HALLAM TUCK ESTATE, Avenue d'Argenteuil, Waterloo, Belgium; 1929–30; (D); extant.

Duer Estate: Courtesy of the Society for the Preservation of Long Island Antiquities, Cold Spring Harbor, New York

BEVERLY DUER ESTATE, Whispering Laurels, Ridge Road, Laurel Hollow, New York; c. 1929; extant.

INDIAN MOUNTAIN SCHOOL, Lakeville, Connecticut; 1928–29; (A); extant.

DAWES HOUSE, KINNAN HOUSE (ALTERED), RAYMOND DAVIS HOUSE AND SIMON JOHN MCPHERSON INFIRMARY, The Lawrenceville School, Lawrenceville, New Jersey; (D); extant.

Coy Dormitory: J. R. Jordan. Delano & Aldrich Collection, Avery Architectural and Fine Arts Library, Columbia University in the City of New York

CHAPEL, COY DORMITORY AND DINING HALL, The Hotchkiss School, Lakeville, Connecticut; 1929–1931; extant.

CAREW TOWER, with Walter W. Ahlschlager, Fifth and Vine Streets, Cincinnati, Ohio; 1929–30; extant.

AMERICAN GOVERNMENT BUILDING, Place de la Concorde, Paris, France; 1929–32; (D); extant.

QUEENS REFORMED CHURCH, parish house, Jamaica Avenue, Queens Village, New York; extant.

DARTINGTON HALL NURSERY SCHOOL, Totnes, Devonshire, England; 1929–31; extant: Aller Park School.

BURDEN MAUSOLEUM, Troy, New York.

1930

Delano elected corresponding member of Academie Des Beaux-Arts, L'Institut de France.

WOODROW WILSON FOUNDATION, interior alterations, 45 East 65th Street, New York City; extant: Institute for Rational Living.

HARRY ROGERS WINTHROP HOUSE, 120 East 78th Street, New York City; extant.

KIPS BAY BOYS CLUB, 301 East 52nd Street, New York City; (A); extant with alterations, apartments.

Hoppin Estate: Courtesy of the Society for the Preservation of Long Island Antiquities, Cold Spring Harbor, New York

G. BEEKMAN HOPPIN ESTATE, Four Winds, Berry Hill Road, Oyster Bay, New York; c. 1930; extant: Mount Saint Ursula Retreat.

CHILD EDUCATION FOUNDATION, 535 East 84th Street, New York City; 1930–31; extant: The Chapin School.

STERLING DIVINITY SCHOOL, Yale University, Prospect Street, New Haven, Connecticut; 1930–32; (D); extant.

CLINTON H. CRANE ESTATE, Crane Road, Cold Spring Harbor, New York; 1930–34; extant.

AUSTEN RIGGS FOUNDATION, Main Street, Stockbridge, Massachusetts; (A); extant: Foundation Inn, Austen Riggs Center.

ALPHA CHI RHO FRATERNITY, Yale University, Park Street, New Haven, Connecticut; (D); extant: Drama Annex.

ALVAH K. LAWRIE ESTATE, Box Hall, Lower Cairo Road and Pine Tree Boulevard, Thomasville, Georgia; 1930–31; extant.

WILLIAM H. FAIN ESTATE, Round Hill Road, Greenwich, Connecticut; c. 1930.

CRESCENT AVENUE PRESBYTERIAN CHURCH, parish house, Watchung Avenue, Plainfield, New Jersey; 1930–31; extant.

JAPANESE EMBASSY, Massachusetts Avenue NW, Washington, D.C.; 1930–31; (D); extant.

THEODORE KIENDL HOUSE, Bronxville, New York; c. 1930.

United States Pavilion: Gacomelli Studio.
Delano & Aldrich Collection, Avery Architectural and Fine Arts Library,
Columbia University in the City of New York

UNITED STATES PAVILION AT THE VENICE BIENNALE, Castello Gardens, Venice, Italy; extant: Solomon R. Guggenheim Foundation.

HENRY EMERSON TUTTLE HOUSE, Ogden Street, New Haven, Connecticut; extant.

FRANK P. WOOD HOUSE, Toronto, Canada; 1930–34.

1931

GEORGE F. BAKER, JR., HOUSE, addition, 67 East 93rd Street, New York City; (D); extant.

HARRY HARKNESS FLAGLER HOUSE, addition, 30 Park Avenue, New York City; (A); demolished.

COLONEL CHARLES A. LINDBERGH ESTATE, Highfields, Lindbergh Road, Hopewell, New Jersey; (A); extant: Albert Elias Residential Group Center.

JOHN DIXON LIBRARY, The Lawrenceville School, Lawrenceville, New Jersey; (D); extant.

MRS. E.V. HARTFORD ESTATE, Wando Plantation, Charleston, South Carolina; (D); destroyed in fire: 1940s.

Pan American Airways System: Prints and Photographs
Division, #303625, Library of Congress

PAN AMERICAN AIRWAYS SYSTEM, TERMINAL BUILDING, Pan American Drive, Dinner Key, Miami, Florida; 1931–34; extant: Miami City Hall.

BOWERS HALL, Yale University, Prospect Street, New Haven, Connecticut; (D); extant.

FIRST CHURCH OF CHRIST SCIENTIST, Dosoris Way and Oak Lane, Glen Cove, New York; extant.

1932

LAWRENCE FARMS HOUSE, Lawrence Park Realty Co., Mount Kisco, New York.

MRS. WILLIAM R. CRAIG ESTATE, Boxwood, Becktown Road, Mocksville, North Carolina; 1932–34; (D): extant.

MONUMENT TO THE CONFEDERATE DEFENDERS OF CHARLESTON, with H. A. MacNeil, White Point Gardens, Charleston, South Carolina; extant.

S. FORRY LAUCKS DAIRY FARM, Lauxmont Dairy, Wrightsville, Pennsylvania; 1932–33; (D); extant.

United States Post Office: Wurts Brothers.
Delano & Aldrich Collection, Avery Architectural and Fine Arts Library,
Columbia University in the City of New York

UNITED STATES POST OFFICE, Glen Cove Avenue, Glen Cove, New York; 1932–33; extant.

1933

MRS. LEWIS ELDRIDGE HOUSE, Redcote, alterations, Bayview Avenue, Great Neck, New York; demolished.

DAVID K. E. BRUCE ESTATE, Staunton Hill, additions to 1848 house and gardens, Route Two, Brookneal, Virginia; extant: inn.

PRINCETON THEOLOGICAL SEMINARY, Miller Chapel, alterations, Princeton, New Jersey; extant.

BUEHLER DORMITORY, The Hotchkiss School, Lakeville, Connecticut; extant.

UNITED STATES DEPARTMENT OF LABOR, Ellis Island, ferry house and storage building, New York City; 1933–36; (A); extant.

1935

Aldrich leaves firm to head the American Academy in Rome.

DAVID STEWART IGLEHART ESTATE, La Granja, Jericho Turnpike, Old Westbury, New York; c. 1935.

JAMES MCV. BREED HOUSE, additions, Amenia, New York.

CONWAY H. OLMSTED ESTATE, Canterbury Road, Lake Bluff, Illinois; c. 1935; extant.

PAN AMERICAN AIRWAYS SYSTEM, terminal building and accommodations, Midway, Wake, and Guam Island; (D); demolished: World War II.

1936

Delano appointed to Board of Design for the 1939 World's Fair (1936–39).

WILLIAMSON S. HOWELL, JR., ESTATE, Villa Maria, Ursuline Avenue, Bryan, Texas; extant: winery and resort.

JEAN WITTOUCK ESTATE, Dennenhuis, Chausee de Bruxelles, Brussels, Belgium; 1936–37; (D); extant.

MONAHAN GYMNASIUM, The Hotchkiss School, Lakeville, Connecticut; 1936–38; extant.

1937

HELEN PORTER PRYIBIL ESTATE, Bogheid, Lattingtown Road, Glen Cove, New York; c. 1937; (D); extant.

Eberstadt Estate: Courtesy of the Society for the Preservation of Long Island Antiquities, Cold Spring Harbor, New York

FERDINAND EBERSTADT ESTATE, Target Rock Farm, Lloyd Harbor Road, Lloyd Neck, New York; (D); demolished: 1995.

CARNEGIE INSTITUTION OF WASHINGTON, addition to Administration Building by Carrère & Hastings, 16 Street and P Street, Washington, D.C.; 1937–38; extant.

NEW YORK MUNICIPAL AIRPORT, with George Licht, LaGuardia Field, Flushing, New York; administration building, marine air terminal, hangars, shops, offices, bulk gasoline storage plant and fuel distribution system, loading platforms, and all utilities (fourteen buildings); 1937–42; (D); extant: marine air terminal, hangars, demolished: main administration building and loading platform in the early 1960s.

PAN AMERICAN AIRWAYS SYSTEM, terminal building, Charleston Airport, Charleston, South Carolina; 1937–38.

MACKENZIE ADMINISTRATION BUILDING, The Lawrenceville School, Lawrenceville, New Jersey; (D); extant.

HIBBS MEMORIAL GYMNASIUM, Hope Farm School, Verbank, New York; 1937–38; extant: Fountains at Millbrook.

1938

BURR MEMORIAL, Hartford Library, Hartford, Connecticut; (D).

ENTRANCE GATES, The Hotchkiss School, Lakeville, Connecticut; extant.

ST. CLARE'S MERCY HOSPITAL, St. John's, Newfoundland, Canada; 1938–39; extant.

1939

Delano awarded an honorary Master's degree from Yale.

GENERAL AND MRS. EDWIN M. WATSON ESTATE, Kenwood, Thomas Jefferson Parkway, Charlottesville, Virginia; (D); 1939–41; extant: International Center for Jefferson Studies.

WORKS PROGRESS ADMINISTRATION, with George Licht, Works Progress Administration Building and Exhibition Building for Hortus, World's Fair, New York.

National Gallery: Delano & Aldrich Collection, Avery Architectural and Fine Arts Library, Columbia University in the City of New York

NATIONAL GALLERY, wing, London, England; 1939–40; (D); never built.

1940

Aldrich dies on December 27, age 69.

PAUL MELLON ESTATE, Brick House at Oak Spring, Upperville, Virginia; (D); extant.

STANLEY WOODWARD ESTATE, Colle, Thomas Jefferson Parkway, Charlottesville, Virginia; (D); extant.

COUNTESS DE TALLEYRAND HOUSE, Pavillon Colombe, alterations, Saint–Brice–sous–Forêt, France; (D); c. 1940; extant.

UNITED STATES NAVY, administration building and storehouse, Balboa, Canal Zone, Panama.

NATIONAL ACADEMY, gallery interiors, 1083 Fifth Avenue, New York City; 1940–42; (D); extant.

UNITED STATES NAVY, special ordinances plant, York, Pennsylvania; c. 1940.

1941

VINCENT D. ANDRUS HOUSE, Windwick, Dairy Road, Greenwich, Connecticut; 1941–42; extant.

CORNELIUS VANDERBILT WHITNEY ESTATE; Wheatley Road, Old Westbury, New York; extant: Old Westbury Golf and Country Club.

MRS. AUDREY PHIPPS HOLDEN HOUSE, alterations, Cascade Road, New Canaan, Connecticut.

WILLIAM HALLAM TUCK HOUSE, Perrywood, alterations, Upper Marlboro, Maryland; extant.

1943

CARTER HIGGINS HOUSE, Westwood Drive, Worcester, Massachusetts; 1943–44; extant.

1945

Firm wins competition for enlarging West Point facilities.

NEW YORK MUNICIPAL AIRPORT, Idlewild, New York, temporary administration building, power house, passenger loading, hangars, shops, and offices; 1945–48; (D); demolished.

BLAIR ACADEMY, auditorium, recreation building, Blairstown, New Jersey; 1945–1950.

UNITED STATES MILITARY ACADEMY, additions to Cadet Hall and Cadet Gymnasium, West Point, New York; plans for new academic building, cadet barracks, nurses' quarters, memorial building, museum: never built.

1946

LILLIAN WALD JUNIOR HIGH SCHOOL #104, New York City; 1946–47.

GEORGE NICHOLS HOUSE, Smith Cottage, alterations, Cold Spring, New York; 1946–47.

1947

FOX HOLLOW SCHOOL, alterations, previously Holmwood (1919), Lenox, Massachusetts; extant: Fox Hollow Resort, altered.

1948

THE WHITE HOUSE, South Portico, Washington, D.C.; (D); extant.

AMERICAN BATTLE MONUMENTS COMMISSION, Epinal American Cemetery and Memorial, with Malvina Hoffman, Epinal, Vosges, France; 1948–56; (D); extant.

PISART MAUSOLEUM, Gate of Heaven Cemetery, Westchester, New York; c. 1948.

1949

Delano appointed architectural consultant to the Commission on the Renovation of the Executive Mansion (1949–52).

THE WHITE HOUSE, structural alterations, Delano as supervisor, Washington, D.C.; 1949–52.

OYSTER BAY FREE PUBLIC LIBRARY, alterations, East Main Street, Oyster Bay, New York; extant.

EDSEL FORD MEMORIAL LIBRARY, The Hotchkiss School, Lakeville, Connecticut; 1949–1952; H. S. Waterbury; extant.

VIRGINIA MILITARY INSTITUTE, expansion program, Lexington, Virginia.

1950

Delano retires as an active partner of the firm and becomes advisory partner.

1953

Delano wins the A.I.A. Gold Medal.

1960

Delano dies on January 12, age 85.

The following projects are listed in the firm's records but are undated.

HOUSES AND ESTATES

ALEXANDER, A. S., Bull's Head, New York

BROKAW, IRVING, DAIRY BUILDING, Mill Neck, New York

BROWN, THATCHER M., New York City

CARLE, ROBERT W., Gaywaring, South Salem, New York

CHAPIN, CHARLES, New York City

CLEWS, MRS. HENRY, alterations, New York City

CROMWELL, SEYMOUR, alterations, Bernardsville, New Jersey.

CUTTING, HON. BRONSON, alterations, Washington, D.C.

DAVIDSON, ARCHIBALD R., Staten Island, New York

DEFOREST MANICE, William, Old Westbury, New York

DREYFUL, L. A., Grimes Hills, New York

EMMONS, K. P., Dongan Hills, Staten Island, New York

FILLEY, MRS. OLIVER D., alterations, New York City

FRASER, JAMES EARLE, New York City

FRIEZE, LYMAN B., JR., Staten Island, New York

GALLOWHUR, WILLIAM GIBSON, Mount Kisco, New York

GARY, MRS. ELBERT H., apartment, New York City

GOODWIN, F. SPENCER, New York City

GUNNISON, FOSTER, Bronxville, New York

HAGUE, MARION, Stockbridge, Massachusetts

HOFMANN, JOSEF, Mont Perelin, Vevey, France

HOUGH, M. L., Rye, New York

KELLEY, NICHOLAS, alterations, New York City

LEACH, HENRY GODDARD, alterations, Villa Nova, Pennsylvania

LLOYD, J. B., Hudson Street, Kinderhook, New York; extant.

MASON, JULIAN S., Pound Hollow Cottage, Glenhead, New York

MONTAGUE, GILBERT H., alterations, New York City

MOORE, CLEMENT C., Greenwich, Connecticut

MOORE, E. C., Cambridge, Massachusetts

MURPHY, GRAYSON M. P., alterations, New York City

PAGE, WALTER H., Cold Spring Harbor, New York

PAYNE, ROBERT G., New York City

PHIPPS, OGDEN, alterations, Roslyn, New York

Pinchot House: Samuel H. Gottscho.
Delano & Aldrich Collection,
Avery Architectural and Fine Arts Library,
Columbia University in the City of New York

PINCHOT, GIFFORD, Southampton, New York

PRATT, JOHN T., tennis court building, Glen Cove, New York

REED, JOSEPH VERNER, apartment, New York City

REED, MRS. VERNER Z., Denver, Colorado; never built.

RHOADS, CHARLES J., alterations, Bryn Mawr, Pennsylvania

ROIG, HAROLD J., Great Neck, New York

RUMBOUGH, STANLEY M., Jr., alterations, Locust Valley, New York

RYAN, CLENDENIN J., Hackettstown, New York; never built.

SAGE, ANDREW G. C., alterations, New York City.

SANDS, MISS ANNA, Wolver Hollow Road, Brookville, New York

THOMPSON, MRS. LEWIS S., alterations, Red Bank, New Jersey and New York City

THOMPSON, DR. WILLIAM PAYNE, Red Bank, New Jersey.

TODD, ROBERT E., THISTLETON, pool and tennis court building, Split Rock Road, Syosset, New York

VANDERBILT, CORNELIUS, alterations, New York City and Newport, Rhode Island

VIETOR, E. G. SOUTHWICK, Greenwich, Connecticut

WHITE, MRS. HENRY, alterations, New York City

WINTHROP, HARRY ROGERS, tennis court building, Cold Spring Harbor, New York

NONRESIDENTIAL PROJECTS

BANK FOR SAVINGS, main office alterations, 72nd Street, New York City

BLESSED SACRAMENT SCHOOL, Delafield Avenue, West Brighton, Staten Island, New York

BLISS MAUSOLEUM, Woodlawn Cemetery, New York City

BROOKVILLE GRADE SCHOOL, Brookville, New York

CHRIST CHURCH, alterations, Main Street, Oyster Bay, New York

FIDUCIARY TRUST COMPANY BANKING QUARTERS, New York City

HANOVER NATIONAL BANK ALTERATIONS, New York City

HILLCREST SCHOOL, Taconic, Connecticut

INTERNATIONAL GRENFELL ASSOCIATION, Newfoundland, Canada

ORPHANAGE AND HOSPITAL, ST. ANTHONY SCHOOL AND HOSPITAL, Northwest River

MECHANICS AND METALS NATIONAL BANK AND OFFICE BUILDING, West 57th Street, New York City

NORRIE MAUSOLEUM, Hyde Park, New York

SCHEEPERS ADMINISTRATION BUILDING, Brookville, New York

SOCIETY GENERALE BANKING QUARTERS, New York City

TRANSIT BUILDING, lobby alterations, 41 East 42nd Street, New York City

VAN CORTLAND BURIAL GROUNDS, enclosure, Van Cortland Park, New York

NOTES

THE ARCHITECTURE OF
DELANO & ALDRICH

1. Kenneth M. Murchison, "Mr. Murchison of New York Says—," *The Architect* 11 (December 1928): 351.
2. "Many Mansions," *Time* 12 (November 12, 1928): 32.
3. As McKim, Mead & White had established a scholarship for Americans to study architecture in Rome, Delano & Aldrich, recognizing the emerging American spirit in architecture, endowed a prize to allow French students to study in the United States. Reported in "Many Mansions," p. 32, "A sum of money, contributed by the guests at the party, was presented by Mrs. Corrine Roosevelt Robinson to the American Institute of Architects to establish a fund to enable French students of architecture to visit the United States to study the work done here, which will help repay, in a small way, the generosity of the French government to the many American students who have received their education, free of charge, at the Ecole des Beaux-Arts in Paris." The fellowship—often referred to as *la Bourse Delano*—is still in existence today.
4. The term "brown decades" was coined by critic Lewis Mumford in his book *The Brown Decades: A Study of Arts in America: 1865–1895*. While the period after the Civil War, leading up to the turn of the century, saw a rise in culture and extraordinary wealth, architecture was increasingly cluttered and somber and dark brownstone was a common material.
5. A 1940 exhibit at the Architectural League, VERSUS, dramatized the ongoing clash of opinion between the traditional and modernist camps. The exhibit, divided into two distinct sections, was organized to promote polemical discussion between the two schools of architecture. During the opening-night dinner, key speakers William Adams Delano and George Howe spoke on the current status of architecture, silhouetted against a great model of McKim, Mead & White's Morgan Library. While more conservative critics, such as Royal Cortissoz, championed the traditionalist content of VERSUS, the modern camp disparaged it and heralded its modernist counterpart. Lewis Mumford wrote, "That there is still any debate about these matters in architectural circles is a sign of curious architectural innocence. . . . On one floor are depicted the dead buildings that were built to resemble other dead buildings. On the upper floor is a vivid array of fresh buildings, evolved freely out of the needs and tastes of our own day." "VS," *Architectural Forum* 72 (April 1940): 15. Delano & Aldrich, however, considered their work modern for the same reasons that Mumford praised the modernist exhibit. They too used "all the new methods of construction and all the new gadgets" (William Adams Delano, "Architecture is an Art," *Architectural Forum* 72 [April 1940]: 16) and believed that if a design was "handled with freedom and . . . answered the needs of our present day clients, it will be really expressive of our own time"—or modern. John Taylor Boyd, "The Classic Spirit in our Country Homes," *Arts & Decoration* 31 (October 1929): 62.
6. Delano, "Architecture is an Art," p. 16.
7. William Adams Delano, "My Architectural Creed," *Pencil Points* 13 (January 10, 1932): 145.
8. Chester Holmes Aldrich, "What is Modern Architecture?" *Architecture* 59 (January 1929): 2.
9. The Delano family descended from Huguenot Philippe de la Noye, as did the Franklin Delano Roosevelts. However, the families were only distantly related. Warren, Frederick A., and Sarah Delano (mother of Franklin Delano Roosevelt) were descendants of Lieutenant Jonathan Delano (1647–1720).

William Adams Delano was descended from an unknown branch of the Delano line, broken or disconnected from the main lines of Delano. Major Joel Andrew Delano, *The Genealogy, History and Alliances of the American House of Delano, 1621–1899*, New York, [n.p.], 1899. The Adams dynasty included two American presidents. Susan Magoun Adams's sister married John Crosby Brown of Brown Brothers & Company.

10. *The Reminiscences of William Adams Delano*, February 1950, page 3 in the Columbia University Oral History Research Office Collection (hereafter CUOHROC).

11. Delano was the eldest of six children. His younger sister Martha died at the age of one. His other siblings were Moreau, Caroline (married to Dr. Augustus Wadsworth), Susan (married to Charles McKelvey), and Eugene. Other neighbors at Orange Mountain included the Douglas Robinsons—Mrs. Douglas Robinson was Theodore Roosevelt's sister.

12. *The Reminiscences of William Adams Delano*, February 1950, page 4 in the CUOHROC. At Yale, Delano studied painting under John Ferguson Weir.

13. *The Reminiscences of William Adams Delano*, February 1950, pages 4–5 in the CUOHROC.

14. William Adams Delano, *A Letter to my Grandson*, New York, 1942, p. 60. Delano & Aldrich Collection, Avery Architectural and Fine Arts Library, Columbia University in the City of New York.

15. Letter from William Adams Delano to Leopold Arnaud, Columbia University, School of Architecture, October 11, 1949. William Adams Delano Papers. Manuscripts and Archives, Yale University Library.

16. For an extensive discussion of Columbia's School of Architecture, see Richard Oliver, *The Making of an Architect, 1881–1981* (New York: Rizzoli, 1981).

17. Letter from William Adams Delano to Leopold Arnaud, Columbia University, School of Architecture, October 11, 1949. William Adams Delano Papers. Manuscripts and Archives, Yale University Library.

18. *The Reminiscences of William Adams Delano*, February 1950, page 6 in the CUOHROC. Maxfield Parrish's poster for the competition was the piece that was actually used by Colgate Perfumes, not Delano's.

19. *The Reminiscences of William Adams Delano*, February 1950, page 6 in the CUOHROC. In his will, Thomas Hastings left funds to correct the portico of the New York Public Library with which

he was displeased. When Hastings died in 1929, his executors turned to Delano for advice on how to apply the bequest. Delano determined that there was not enough money to make the improvements and directed the funds to be split between Yale and Harvard.

20. *The Reminiscences of William Adams Delano*, February 1950, page 7 in the CUOHROC.

21. Delano, *A Letter to my Grandson*, pp. 33–34. According to Delano, only ten foreigners were admitted to the Ecole per year. In the entrance examinations, mathematics and architecture were most important while drawing, modeling, and history were given less weight.

22. William Adams Delano, "A Marriage of Convenience," *Journal of the A.I.A.* 1 (May 1944): 221.

23. At the Ecole, students entered the second class and were admitted to the first class once they obtained the necessary honorable mentions and values required to advance. Medals and mentions were conferred through monthly competitions during which the ateliers worked against one another. If a student was awarded a mention or a medal, it reflected well on all of the students in the atelier. Delano entered the second class at the Ecole in 1899 and was promoted to the first class in 1901. He won three medals in the second class and six in the first. The Laloux atelier was an *atelier libre*. It was privately run as opposed to the *ateliers officiels* (of which there were three) that were housed in the Ecole's school buildings. Laloux's studio was located at 8 rue d'Assis.

24. Misc. Mss. Aldrich, Chester Holmes. Courtesy of The New-York Historical Society.

25. Interview with J. Winthrop Aldrich, April 2002.

26. Although foreigners were not eligible for the Prix de Rome, students gravitated towards the higher caliber ateliers known for winning the prize. Aldrich entered the second class at the Ecole in 1895 and was promoted to the first class in 1897. He won seven medals in the second class and seven in the first class. Pierre Esquié became the *patron* of the Daumet-Girault-Esquié atelier in 1888, an *atelier libre* located at 15 rue de Buci. Honoré Daumet had founded the atelier in 1860 and Charles Girault took it over in 1885. Esquié was from Toulouse and was known for his designs for the Ecole des Beaux Arts and the Salle de Fetes et Capitole in that city. Other American students in the Esquié atelier included Joseph H. Freedlander, Joseph Howland Hunt (son of Richard Morris Hunt), and Charles Cogswell from Boston.

27. William Adams Delano, "To be an Ideal Architect," *Pencil Points* 13 (February 1932): 106.

28. Delano, *A Letter to my Grandson*, p. 56. President Roosevelt's sister, Corinna Roosevelt Robinson, had been Delano's neighbor in Orange Mountain; they were great friends.

29. Edward Potter is best known for his design for the Mark Twain house in Nook Farm, Hartford, Connecticut, and numerous designs for the Episcopal Church.

30. Delano's *A Letter to my Grandson* (and namesake) was written in 1942. A copy of this letter is in the Delano & Aldrich Collection, Avery Architectural and Fine Arts Library, Columbia University in the City of New York.

31. When Aldrich moved to Rome, Amey accompanied him and acted as the unofficial hostess of the Villa Aurelia at the American Academy; after her brother's death in 1940, she filled his place until the academy was closed in 1941 for the duration of World War II.

32. "Studio for Delano & Aldrich, 126 East 38th Street, New York City," *Architecture* 35 (June 1917): 111–14; Everett D. Waid, "How Architects Work," *The Brickbuilder* 21 (February 1912): 35–38.

33. *The Reminiscences of William Adams Delano*, February 1950, pages 18–19 in the CUOHROC.

34. *The Reminiscences of William Adams Delano*, February 1950, pages 90–93 in the CUOHROC. Delano and Aldrich chose the order of the firm's name by tossing a coin. Delano's name came up on top three times consecutively. Josephine Manning, Delano's loyal secretary and stenographer, came to the firm in 1916 and continued as Delano's personal secretary until his death in 1960.

35. Interview with David Aldrich, August 2001, Providence, Rhode Island. George A. Licht was the first winner of the Paris Prize, one of the most eagerly sought out awards in American Architecture that was established in 1904 by the Society of Beaux-Arts Architects. At this time, Licht was studying under Joseph Freedlander who had established an atelier in New York on his return from the Ecole des Beaux-Arts. In 1905, after winning the Paris Prize, Licht entered directly into the first class at the Ecole where he received eleven medals. He also established an atelier in New York. Herbert Godwin graduated from the Columbia School of Architecture, Henry S. Waterbury studied architecture in Buffalo, New York and in Paris, and James Stewardson was a British architect. Licht and Waterbury's sons—George T. Licht and John W. Waterbury—as well as Delano's nephew through marriage, Alexander McIlvaine, later became associates of the firm.

36. The Coffee House was created as an informal organization, which Delano described as the "junior Century Club." The club was founded by Delano, Frank Crowninshield, founding editor of *Vanity Fair*; Henry Gray; and Rawlins Cottenet. The club, which resided in rented rooms at the Hotel Seymour at 54 West 45th Street, had no rules and consisted mainly of artists, architects, and writers. Aldrich and Grosvenor Atterbury started the Digressionists, a small club of architects, in 1904. An annual dinner was held during which the members exhibited their work.

37. In 1903, Professor A. D. F. Hamlin, Columbia's director of architecture (instated after Ware's retirement) asked Delano to head one of the school's newly established ateliers. While Delano had been discouraged by his Columbia experience, he thought the school's new direction emphasizing design, renderings, and healthy competition a promising development. Three ateliers were established initially. Delano was in charge of the uptown drafting room while Charles McKim and Thomas Hastings, with respective associates John Russell Pope and H. W. Corbett, ran the downtown studios. According to Delano's university record, he served as "tutor in drawing and design" from 1903 to 1906 and "associate director of atelier" from 1906 to 1911.

38. *The Reminiscences of William Adams Delano*, February 1950, pages 9–10 in the CUOHROC.

39. Remarks made by The Honorable Learned Hand at Delano's memorial service held on February 1, 1960, at the Brick Presbyterian Church, New York City. William Adams Delano Papers. Manuscripts and Archives, Yale University Library.

40. Delano, *A Letter to my Grandson*, p. 45.

41. "Chester Holmes Aldrich." William Adams Delano Papers. Manuscripts and Archives, Yale University Library.

42. Royal Cortissoz, "Chester Aldrich," in the Chester and Amey Aldrich scrapbooks at Rokeby, Barrytown, New York.

43. As recorded by an alumni questionnaire from Columbia, Aldrich's hobbies were "water coloring and music," his recreation "walking in the Alps." Letter from Chester H. Aldrich to Daniel C. McCarthy, assistant editor, *Columbia Alumni News*, March 23, 1943, Biographical Files, Columbia University Archives, Columbiana Library. Delano, during the later years of his life, often lamented that he did not have hobbies

with which to keep busy. He was, however, a voracious reader and a prolific writer of letters, articles, and verse, including a volume called *Random Rhymes*, June 1952. A copy of *Random Rhymes* is in the William Adams Delano papers. Manuscripts and Archives, Yale University Library.

44. Misc. Mss. Aldrich, Chester Holmes. Courtesy of The New-York Historical Society.

45. Delano, *A Letter to my Grandson*, p. 45.

46. "C. H. Aldrich Dies; Noted Architect," *The New York Times* (December 27, 1940): p. 19.

47. Chester Aldrich's speech given at the firm's twentieth anniversary party. The Chester and Amey Aldrich scrapbooks at Rokeby, Barrytown, New York.

48. As discussed in Robert A. M. Stern, Gregory Gilmartin, and John Massingale, *New York 1900: Metropolitan Architecture and Urbanism, 1890–1915* (New York: Rizzoli, 1983), the age of metropolitanism extended from after the Civil War to 1940. During this period, cities grew dramatically as a reflection of the period's progressive and optimistic nature.

49. An extended discussion regarding the development of the American country house can be found in Mark Alan Hewitt's *The Architect and the American Country House 1890–1940* (New Haven: Yale University Press, 1990).

50. *Country Life* 46 (August 1924); *Country Life* 46 (October 1924); "Distinguished architects who have made a specialty of designing successful country houses," *Country Life* 37 (April 1920): 142.

51. Royal Cortissoz, *Portraits of Ten Country Houses Designed by Delano & Aldrich* (Garden City, N.Y.: Doubleday, Page & Company), pp. viii–x.

52. An extensive discussion of the development of the Upper East Side and the various types of residential buildings can be found in Stern et el., *New York 1900*, pp. 306–436. According to *New York 1900*, Carrère & Hastings's residence for Senator Root at 71st Street and Park Avenue (1903–5), a brick mansion in a Georgian Revival style animated by contrasting limestone trim and textured brickwork, was the firm's simplest design to date; the fact that such a prominent figure would build such a house impressed itself upon society's sensibilities and impacted the form and style of residential building thereafter.

53. Susan Stiles Dowell, "Rebirth in Baltimore: Restoration of the Walters Art Gallery," *Southern Accents* 12 (January–February 1989): 54–60; "The Walters Museum, Baltimore, Md. Delano & Aldrich, Architects," *Architectural Review* 17, 3 (1910): pls. 21, 22, 27; Francis Henry Taylor, "The Walters Gallery Revisited," *Parnassus* 6 (December 1934): 1–6, 31; William R. Johnston, *William and Henry Walters, the Reticent Collectors* (Baltimore, Md.: John Hopkins University Press, 1999), pp. 163–69.

54. Delano, *Letter to my Grandson*, p. 43.

55. Hugh J. McCauley, "Visions of Kykuit: John D. Rockefeller's House at Pocantico Hills, Tarrytown, NY," *The Hudson Valley Regional Review: A Journal of Regional Studies* 10 (September 1993): 1–51; Anne Rockefeller Roberts, *The Rockefeller Family Home: Kykuit* (New York: Abbeville Press, 1998); "The Country Home of John D. Rockefeller, Esq.," *The House Beautiful* 26 (June 1909): 1–9. The architects were never to mention the commission in articles or reminiscences.

56. Delano & Aldrich, *For You to Decide* (New York: privately printed, n.d.). A copy of *For You to Decide* is in the Delano & Aldrich Collection, Avery Architectural and Fine Arts Library, Columbia University in the City of New York.

57. Delano & Aldrich, *For You to Decide*.

58. A. Lawrence Kocher, "The Country House: An Analysis of the Architect's Method of Approach," *Architectural Record* 62 (November 1927): 342.

59. Kocher, "The Country House," p. 342.

60. Delano, *A Letter to my Grandson*, p. 43.

61. The Brick House (1940), on the Mellons' five-thousand-acre horse farm, was Delano's last great house commission. Mellon, who had admired the Georgian style of William Buckland's Hammond-Harwood House in Annapolis (1774) when he attended St. John's College, suggested this model to the architect (Paul Mellon with John Baskett, *Reflections in a Silver Spoon* [New York: William Morrow, 1992], p. 226). While the Brick House faithfully reproduced the essential massing and character of the Annapolis prototype, the rich exterior details were almost nonexistent. Delano did produce some of the elaborate carving and decoration on the interiors of the house, such as in the drawing room which is a full copy of the rich paneled original. The portico at the Mellon house has a plain frieze and a simple keystone, while the Hammond-Harwood House had sophisticated carvings of swags on its portico, ornament on its frieze, and decoration. Though much more sparing than the Hammond-Harwood House in its detail, the Mellon house still reflects the elegant hand of its architect.

62. Boyd, "The Classic Spirit in our Country Homes," p. 59.

63. Delano & Aldrich, *For You to Decide*.

64. Augusta Owen Patterson referred to these painted rooms as "decorative rooms" and observed that they were "a proper work of art rather than of architecture." Augusta Owen Patterson, *American Homes of To-day* (New York: Macmillan, 1924), p. 387. Other articles on the firm's interiors include Helen Churchill Candee, "Interior Decoration: Some Domestic Interiors from the Work of Delano & Aldrich," *Architectural Forum* 32 (June 1920): 225–30; "Mural Painting for Minor Buildings," *Architectural Forum* 34 (May 1921); Howard Major, "Adapting the Eighteenth Century Interior," *Architectural Forum* 36 (June 1922): 247–52; Horace Mann, "A Plea for the Architect's Interest in Textile Fabrics," *Architectural Forum* 37 (October 1922): 199–202.

65. Alexander King, "Traditional Forms of Electric Lighting," *Architecture* 49 (March 1924): 73–76, 82. In the drawings for the Knickerbocker Club, the stone carver was directed to refer to the architect's full-scale models for the sculptural details. The firm often used Foster Gunnison to execute light-fixture designs. In the 1940s, Gunnison gave Delano two bound volumes into which he had pasted all of Delano's original sketches for fixtures. The location of these volumes is unknown.

66. William Adams Delano, "Further Thoughts on Contemporary Architecture," *Pencil Points* 13 (July 1932): 468.

67. Delano, "Further Thoughts on Contemporary Architecture," p. 468.

68. Boyd, "The Classic Spirit in our Country Homes," p. 62.

69. This element, particularly in the firm's house designs, became increasingly pronounced in its later work. The design of the Charles S. Payson house (1927–28) in the Whitney family compound in Manhasset, Long Island reflected the family's love of hunting. Fox heads, horns, and other emblems of the hunt were incorporated into the window grilles, lighting fixtures, mantels, and moldings; old hunting murals adorned the breakfast room walls. At Dennenhuis (House of the Pine Trees) for Jean Wittouck in Brussels (1936–37), a pine motif was used throughout. The corners of the shutters were pierced with pine trees motifs, pinecones were carved into the stone above the garden door, and the main stair rail was wrought in the shape of trees.

70. Kocher, "The Country House," p. 342. Such labeling seemed unavoidable during this revivalist period. Architectural styles carried a certain weight and appeal for Americans searching for a means of expressing their stature and position. Architects and critics of the era, such as Charles S. Keefe, Aymar Embury, Augusta Owen Patterson, and Samuel Howe, who produced books on the subject of the American country house, often organized the houses around firm stylistic categories. Magazines, according to Aldrich, "labeling American designs as Cotswold, Norman, Georgian, etc.," were just as guilty. Boyd, "The Classic Spirit in our Country Homes," p. 62.

71. William Adams Delano, "Memoirs of Centurian Architects: Part I," *Journal of the A.I.A.* 10 (July 1948): 8.

72. William Adams Delano, "Memoirs of Centurian Architects: Part II," *Journal of the A.I.A.* 10 (August 1948): 81.

73. In his book *The Pageant of America: The American Spirit in Architecture*, Talbot Faulkner Hamlin describes Delano & Aldrich's house for Miss E. R. Hooker, a simple brick and stucco cottage, as a "house of nonstylistic design." He writes, "the trend toward free, nonstylistic design, as opposed to historical or even eclectic design is bound to influence profoundly future American architecture in America. All the beauty of this house is due to its proportion and its material—the careful relationship of all its parts." Talbot Faulkner Hamlin, *The Pageant of America: The American Spirit in Architecture* (New Haven, Conn.: Yale University Press, 1926), p. 330.

74. Boyd, "The Classic Spirit in our Country Homes," p. 62.

75. An extended discussion of the Muttontown enclave can be found in Mark Alan Hewitt, "Domestic Portraits: The Early Long Island Country Houses of Delano & Aldrich," in *Long Island Architecture* (Interlaken, N.Y.: Heart of the Lakes Publishing, 1991), pp. 99–115; and Mark Alan Hewitt, "William Adams Delano and the Muttontown Enclave," *Antiques* 132 (August 1997): 316–27. For additional Long Island houses, see Richard Guy Wilson, "Delano & Aldrich," in Robert B. MacKay, Anthony K. Baker, and Carol A. Traynor, *Long Island Country Houses and Their Architects, 1860–1940* (New York: Norton, 1997), pp. 127–43.

76. "House, Egerton L. Winthrop, Syosset, Long Island," *Architecture* 41 (April 1920): pls. 54–57; Samuel Howe, "The Country House of Mr. E. L. Winthop, Jr.," *Town & Country* 69 (November 14, 1914): 16–17; "House of Egerton L. Winthrop, Jr., Esq., Syosset, L.I., N.Y.," *The American Architect* 108 (July 28, 1915); "A Comely House on Long Island, at Syosset," *Town & Country* 78 (May 20, 1921): 30–31; Cortissoz, *Portraits of Ten Country Houses*, pp. 50–54;

Samuel Howe, *American Country Houses of To-day* (New York: Architectural Book Publishing, 1915), pp. 240–45; Patterson, *American Homes of To-day*, pp. 27, 188–89. Muttontown Meadows was actually built for Bronson, who turned it over to his brother, Egerton, when he commissioned a new and larger house by Delano & Aldrich in 1910.

77. "House of Mr. W. A. Delano, Esq., Syosset, L.I., N.Y.," *The American Architect* 107 (May 12, 1915); Samuel Howe, "Mr. William Adams Delano's Home at Brookville," *Town & Country* 69 (October 31, 1914): 15–16, 30; Howe, *American Country Houses of To-day*, pp. 14–19; "A House in an Apple Orchard, The Home of Wm. Adams Delano at Syosset, L.I.," *Country Life* 34 (May 1918): 68–69; Cortissoz, *Portraits of Ten Country Houses*, pp. 55–61; Wilson, "Delano & Aldrich," p. 137–38.

78. Cortissoz, *Portraits of Ten Country Houses*, p. xi.

79. One friend recalled that the Prince of Wales, on his 1924 trip to the North Shore, had visited Delano's house to watch the French-inspired game. Interview with Frances Murer, April 26, 2001.

80. "House for Bronson Winthrop, Esq., Syosset, L.I., New York," *The American Architect* 108 (July 7, 1915); Howe, *American Country Houses of To-day*, pp. 4–13; Samuel Howe, "Mr. Bronson Winthrop's Home Near Syosset," *Town & Country* 69 (December 5, 1914): 24–25, 52; Cortissoz, *Portraits of Ten Country Houses*, pp. 44–49; Wilson, "Delano & Aldrich." p. 136.

81. "House of George Whitney, Esq., Westbury, Long Island, N. Y.," *The Architectural Forum* 29 (July 1918): pls. 11–12; E. W. Howell, *Noted Long Island Homes* (Babylon, N.Y.: E. W. Howell, 1933); "Residence of Vincent Astor, Esq., Port Washington, L. I.," *The Architectural Record* 60 (November 1926): 422–24; "House for Vincent Astor, Esq., Port Washington, L. I.," *Architectural League of New York Yearbook* (1926); "A House in Newport, Rhode Island," *The House Beautiful* 55 (February 1924): 142–4; "House of Miss E. R. Hooker, New Haven, Conn.," *The Architectural Forum* 29 (July 1918): pl. 2.

82. Howe, *American Country Houses of To-day*, pp. 192–96; "House at Lenox, Mass., Delano & Aldrich, Architects," *The Brickbuilder* 21 (February 1912): pls. 20–22; Patterson, *American Homes of To-day*, pp. 43, 112–13.

83. Howe, *American Country Houses of To-day*, pp. 118–23; "A House at Mount Kisco, Delano & Aldrich, Architects," *Architectural Record* 30 (October 1911): 353–60; Mac Griswold and Eleanor Weller, *The Golden Age of American Gardens, 1890–1940* (New York: Abrams, 1991), pp. 78–79; "House at Mount Kisco, N.Y.," *The Brickbuilder* 21 (January 1912): pls. 12–13; "Swimming Pool at Mt. Kisco, N.Y.," *The American Architect* 117 (April 7, 1920): 436; "House at Mount Kisco, N.Y.," *Architectural League of New York Yearbook* (1912); "Architecture's Portfolio of Garden Pools," *Architecture* 59 (June 1929): 381, 388.

84. Linda Nochlin, "High Bohemia," *House & Garden* 157 (September 1985): 180–89, 234–36; Ada Rainey, "Mrs. Harry Payne Whitney's Studio at Roslyn," *Town & Country* 69 (March 21, 1914): 31–33, 62; "Studio and Garden for Mrs. Harry Payne Whitney, Wheatley Hills, L.I.," *Architectural Review* 8 (January 1919): 4–5; Jessie Martin Breese, "Adventuring in Studios," *Country Life* 37 (February 1920): 25–39; Monica Randall, *Mansions of Long Island's Gold Coast* (New York: Rizzoli, 1987), pp. 143–46; Griswold and Weller, *The Golden Age of American Gardens, Proud Owners, Private Estates*, pp. 102–3; G. H. Edgell, *The American Architecture of To-Day* (New York: Scribners, 1928), pp. 133–35; Coy Ludwig, *Maxfield Parrish* (New York: Watson-Guptill, 1972), pp. 160–63; Wilson, "Delano & Aldrich," pp. 136–37; Cortissoz, *Portraits of Ten Country Houses*, pp. 38–43; Patterson, *American Homes of To-day*, pp. 9, 146, 398; "Architecture's Portfolio of Garden Pools," *Architecture* 59 (June 1929): 382; Ruth Dean, *The Livable House: Its Garden* (New York: Moffat Yard, 1917), pp. 103, 162.

85. Arthur Drexler, *The Architecture of the Ecole des Beaux-Arts* (Cambridge, Mass.: MIT Press, 1977), p. 489; Charles S. Keefe, ed., *The American House* (New York: UPC Book Company, 1922), p. 13; Dorothy Nicholas, "A Great American Garden," *Country Life* 79 (April 1941): 24–27; Patterson, *American Homes of To-day*, pp. 91, 96–99, 116, 120; "James A. Burden's Residence," *Country Life* 38 (May 1920): 58–60; "House at Syosset, Long Island, New York," *The American Architect* 117 (April 7, 1920); "Residence, James A. Burden, Syosset, Long Island," *Architecture* 41 (March 1920): pls. 39–47; Cortissoz, *Portraits of Ten Country Houses*, pp. 1–7; Wilson, "Delano & Aldrich," pp. 141–42; "If you plan to build in brick," *House & Garden* 46 (October 1924): 92–93.

86. Patterson, *American Homes of To-day*, p. 89.

87. Augusta Owen Patterson, "Mr. Otto H. Kahn's Long Island Residence," *Town & Country* 77 (October 10, 1920): 31–34;

Town & Country 77 (September 20, 1920): 30; Edgell, *The American Architecture of To-day*, pp. 133–34; Patterson, *American Homes of To-day*, pp. 17, 31, 174–80, 293, 341; Randall, *Mansions of Long Island's Gold Coast*, pp. 229–32; "Castles from the Air: the Influence of the French Chateau on American Country Houses," *Country Life* 39 (December 1920): 48–50; Robert B. King, *Raising a Fallen Treasure: the Otto H. Kahn Home* (Mattituck, N.Y.: Mad Printer of Mattituck, 1985); Cortissoz, *Portraits of Ten Country Houses*, pp. 18–28; Wilson, "Delano & Aldrich," pp. 138–40.

88. *The Reminiscences of William Adams Delano*, February 1950, page 31 in the CUOHROC. Otto Kahn was both of the establishment and an outsider. As a financier and partner at Kuhn, Loeb and Co. he was extraordinarily successful, but his liberal social views were anathema to more conservative Wall Street titans like J. P. Morgan. A prominent cultural leader, Kahn led New Yorkers in such efforts as saving the Metropolitan Opera Company, but as a Jew he was isolated from the Protestant establishment. Though Kahn was president of the Metropolitan Opera Company, he was not given a box at the opera until late in his life.

89. "Country Houses of Character," *Country Life* 37 (November 1919): 24, 26; "Dining Room, House at Oyster Bay, Long Island," *The Architectural Forum* 34 (May 1921): pl. 76; Randall, *Mansions of Long Island's Gold Coast*, pp. 212–17; P. H. Elwood, Jr., ed., *American Landscape Architecture* (N.Y.: Architectural Book Publishing, 1924), p. 179; Wilson, "Delano & Aldrich," pp. 140–41; "House at Oyster Bay, L.I., N.Y.," *The American Architect* 117 (April 7, 1920); Cortissoz, *Portraits of Ten Country Houses*, pp. 8–14. Patterson, *American Homes of To-day*, pp. 156–57, 314, 392.

90. "Chelsea," *Harper's Bazaar* (September 1951): 199; "Chelsea Estate: A Brief History," Nassau County Museum; Howell, *Noted Long Island Homes*.

91. *The Reminiscences of William Adams Delano*, February 1950, pages 34–35 in the CUOHROC.

92. "Antiques in American Homes, The Home of Mr. And Mrs. Chalmers Wood," *Antiques* 43 (March 1943): 124–25; Howell, *Noted Long Island Homes*; Wilson, "Delano & Aldrich," p. 143. After ghostwriting Elsie de Wolfe's *The House in Good Taste*, Ruby Ross Wood wrote her own book on decorating entitled *The Honest House*. Wood's color sense, faith in simple forms, and whimsical touch were apparent at Little Ipswich, as they were in other commissions she completed in Palm Beach for the John Vietors, H. Mercer Walkers, and Wolcott Blairs.

93. Howell, *Noted Long Island Homes*; "Country Living in the U.S.A.: Oak Point," *House & Garden* (June 1949). The Williams tore down their big house and converted the tennis court building and pool house into living space in the 1940s. The swimming pool was covered over, creating a 70-foot by 20-foot living room; the tennis court was turned into an indoor garden, and the dressing rooms into bedrooms. Halls were decorated with murals by José Maria Sert.

94. "House at Greenwood, Va., Delano & Aldrich, Architects," *The American Architect* 131 (March 5, 1927): 289; Robert Becker, *Nancy Lancaster: her Life, her Work, her Art* (New York: Knopf, 1996), pp. 105–36; "Mirador, the House of Mrs. Ronald Tree, Greenwood, Va.," *Southern Architect* 54 (June 1928): 41–46; Griswold and Weller, *The Golden Age of American Gardens*, pp. 192–94.

95. Peterloon: "John J. Emery, Residence, Montgomery, Ohio," publication unknown. Delano & Aldrich Collection, Avery Architectural and Fine Arts Library, Columbia University in the City of New York; *From Camargo to Indian Hill* (Indian Hill, Ohio: Indian Hill Historical Museum Association, 1983), pp. 44–47; Walter E. Langsam, *Great Houses of the Queen City* (Cincinnati, Ohio: Cincinnati Historical Society, 1997); "Peterloon: History and Tour," Peterloon Foundation; "Peterloon: Home of John J. Emery Family, Indian Hill, Ohio," Peterloon Foundation.
Tuck estate: Delano & Aldrich Collection, Avery Architectural and Fine Arts Library, Columbia University in the City of New York. One Emery descendant who grew up at Peterloon later lived in Brussels. She came across the Tuck estate accidentally and was shocked by the similarities of the two designs. Apparently when designing the Tucks' house, Delano asked the Emerys if he could use their house as a model.

96. Delano & Aldrich Collection, Avery Architectural and Fine Arts Library, Columbia University in the City of New York. In some of the firm's later houses, such as Kenwood and the nearby Colle (1940), commissioned by Stanley Woodward, Chief of Protocol in the State Department, Delano placed a silver disk on the newel post of the stair engraved with the name of the client, the date, and his own name.

97. "The Rebuilding of Park Avenue," *Real Estate Record and Guide* 84 (December 4, 1909): pp. 991–93.

98. "Millions Spent on East Side Last Year in Home Building Despite Fine Flats to

Lure the Wealthy," *The Sun* (January 30, 1916), section 7, p. 2. In 1915, there were 45 costly dwellings constructed or altered north of 60th Street and east of Central Park.

99. Delano & Aldrich also performed a series of brownstone renovations, transforming high-stooped, architecturally indistinct row houses into historically inspired American basement houses. Brownstone stoops were removed and the front door was relocated to the sidewalk level, the front facades were moved out to the lot line, and the interiors were reorganized accordingly. Residences for Marshall Dodge at 37 East 68th Street (1913) and Elbridge Stratton at 11 East 61st Street (1923) are examples of such conversions.

100. *The American Architect* 107 (March 10, 1915).

101. According to Delano, the Brewster house was the first and only building of his design that he saw demolished during his lifetime. *The Reminiscences of William Adams Delano*, February 1950, page 53 in the CUOHROC.

102. William Adams Delano, "No. 100 East Seventieth Street," *The New York Architect* 2 (June 1908).

103. "Club House Buildings," *Architecture and Building* 47 (December 1915): 427–55; "Current Building Operations: New Homes of the Colony and Knickerbocker Clubs Represent the Best in Modern Building Practice," *Real Estate Record and Guide* 96 (October 23, 1915): 708; "Establishing New Club House Centre in Upper Fifth Avenue District," *The New York Times*, section 8 (January 17, 1915): 3; "The New Home of the Knickerbocker Club," *Vanity Fair* 3 (February 1915): 52; New York Landmarks Preservation Commission, *Knickerbocker Club, 2 East 62nd Street, Borough of Manhattan* (New York: Landmarks Preservation Commission, 1979); Barbaralee Diamondstein, *The Landmarks of New York* (New York: Abrams, 1988), p. 322; Alan Burnham, *New York Landmarks* (Middletown, Conn.: Wesleyan University Press, 1963): p. 266; William J. Dunn, *Knickerbocker Centennial: 1871–1971* (New York: Knickerbocker Club, 1971).

104. "Club House Buildings," *Architecture and Building* 47 (December 1915): 429; "Colony Club, Park Avenue and 62nd Street, New York," *Architecture* 33 (April 1916): pls. 59–73; "Decorations by Robert W. Chanler in the Loggia of the New Home of the Colony Club," *The Sun* (January 30, 1916), section 5, p. 8; "Plans for Colony Club," *The New York Times* (September 18, 1914): 11; "The New Home for the Colony Club,"

Vogue (September 1916): 74–75; "Current Building Operations, New Homes of the Colony and Knickerbocker Clubs Represent the Best in Modern Building Practice," *Real Estate Record and Guide* 96 (October 23, 1915): 708; Frederick James Gregg, "The Bird Loggia of the New Colony Club," *Vanity Fair* 6 (April 1916): 50.

105. "The New Home for the Colony Club," *Vogue*. Robert Winthrop Chanler was a good friend of Gertrude Vanderbilt Whitney, a member of the Colony Club. The frescos in the loggia are actually Chanler's second go-round; he was dissatisfied with his first effort, which was fully executed and accepted by the club and the architects. The second time, Chanler made the frescos less formal and balanced and more colorful and lively. With extensive illustrations and color plates, Ivan Narodny's *The Art of Robert Winthrop Chanler* (New York: William Helburn, 1922) vividly discusses the symbolism and creative genius behind the artist's work.

106. "Distinction in Architecture," *The Architect and Building News* 122 (November 29, 1929): 670.

107. Christopher Gray, "Streetscapes: 1915 Straight Residence, Until Recently the International Center of Photography," *The New York Times*, section 9 (October 14, 2001), p. 9; "Residence, Mrs. Willard Straight, 1130 Fifth Avenue, New York," *Architecture* 41 (March 1920): pls. 33–38; Alexander King, "Traditional Forms of Lighting," *Architecture* 49 (March 1924): 73–82; New York Landmarks Preservation Commission, *National Audubon Society (formerly the Willard Straight House), 1130 Fifth Avenue, Borough of Manhattan* (New York: Landmarks Preservation Commission, 1968); Patterson, *American Homes of To-day*, pp. 104–5, 373–74, 397; Andrew Dolkart, *Touring the Upper East Side: Walks in Five Historic Districts* (New York: New York Landmarks Conservancy, 1995), p. 96; Burnham, *New York Landmarks*, p. 264; Diamondstein, *The Landmarks of New York*, p. 323; New York Landmarks Commission, *Expanded Carnegie Hill Historic District Designation Report* (New York: Landmark Preservation Commission, 1993), p. 82.

108. Stern et al., *New York 1900*, p. 355; "Residence for William Sloane, Esq., Delano & Aldrich, Architects," *Architectural Review* 8 (January 1919): 8–9, pls. 11–14.

109. "The R. Fulton Cutting Group, Houses, 12, 14, 16 East 89th Street, New York City," *The Architect* 4 (August 1925): pls. 116–17.

110. Ann E. Berman, "Past Perfect in New York City," *Architectural Digest* 57 (March 2000): 190–96, 206; "Residence for Francis F. Palmer Esq., 1180 Park Avenue, New York," *Architectural Review* 8 (February 1919): pls. 17–21; *House Beautiful* 53 (May 1923): 476; "A Little Portfolio of Good Interiors," *House & Garden* 35 (June 1919): 43–45; "The Architectural Bookcase," *House & Garden* 35 (June 1919): 35; Diamondstein, *The Landmarks of New York*, p. 332; Christopher Gray, "Streetscapes: the Baker Mansion on Park at 93rd," *The New York Times*, section 10 (October 22, 1989), p. 12; *Expanded Carnegie Hill Historic District Designation Report*, pp. 228–31; New York Landmarks Preservation Commission, *The Synod of Bishops of the Russian Orthodox Church Outside of Russia (formerly George F. Baker, Jr. House) Designation Report* (New York: Landmarks Preservation Commission, 1969); New York Landmarks Preservation Commission, *69 East 93rd Street Designation Report* (New York: Landmarks Preservation Commission, 1969); New York Landmarks Preservation Commission, *67 East 93rd Street Designation Report* (New York: Landmarks Preservation Commission, 1974); Richard Hampton Jenrette, *Adventures with Old Houses* (Charleston, S.C.: Wyrick & Company, 2000),: pp. 146–75; Dolkart, *Touring the Upper East Side*, pp. 92–93.

111. "The Residence of William Woodward, Esq., New York City, Delano & Aldrich, Architects," *Architectural Review* 8 (April 1919): 103–4, pls. 59–60; *Expanded Carnegie Hill Historic District Designation Report*, pp. 126–27; Dolkart, *Touring the Upper East Side*, p. 78.

112. "Residence, Harold I. Pratt, Park Avenue, New York, *Architecture* 46 (July 1922): pls. 104–8; Alexander King, "Traditional Forms of Lighting," *Architecture* 49 (March 1924): 73–82; Edgell, *The American Architecture of To-day*, pp. 141–42; Patterson, *American Homes of To-day*, p. 372.

113. "Boys' Club Building Wins Award," *The New York Times* (May 17, 1931), section 11, p. 11; "Architectural News in Photographs," *Architecture* 62 (July 1930): 14; "Nightingale School, East 92nd Street, New York City," *Architecture* 61 (May 1930): 275.

114. "Current Building Operations," *Real Estate Record and Guide* 95 (May 9, 1914): 838-39; Arthur Loring Bruce, "An Ideal Settlement House," *Vanity Fair* 9 (February 1918): 50, 72; "Wall Paintings in the New Greenwich House," *Town & Country* 73 (February 1, 1918): 33; "Greenwich House, New York City," *Architectural Record* 45 (June 1919): 533, 541; "Greenwich House, New York City, Delano & Aldrich, Architects," *Architectural Forum* 31 (1919): 92, pls. 43–46; Alan Axelrod, ed., *The Colonial Revival in America* (New York: Norton, 1985), pp. 347–48.

115. "The Union Club, Park Avenue and 69th Street, New York, Delano & Aldrich, Architects," *American Architect* 148 (April 1936): 27–38; "Walls that Strike a Decorative Note," *The New York Times,* section 6 (October 22, 1933), p. 14; Reginald Townsend, *Mother of Clubs* (New York: W. E. Rudge, 1936), pp. 100–9; *Herald Tribune*, section 6 (April 5, 1936), p. 1; "Special Report of the Governors of the Union Club to the Members, 1926," Delano & Aldrich Collection, Avery Architectural and Fine Arts Library, Columbia University in the City of New York; "Architectural News in Photographs," *Architecture* 68 (September 1933): 155; "Mr. Murchison of New York Says," *The Architect* 2 (December 1928): 351; "Another Fifth Avenue Change," *Real Estate Record and Guide* 120 (November 19, 1927): 5–6; Dolkart, *Touring the Upper East Side*, p. 47.

116. William Adams Delano, "Artist and Artisan," *Journal of the A.I.A.* 9 (August 1921): 261.

117. Delano spoke of New York Hospital in a letter to Mr. Daniel Schwarz, *The New York Times*, February 28, 1947. William Adams Delano Papers. Manuscripts and Archives, Yale University Library.

118. *The Reminiscences of William Adams Delano*, February 1950, page 54 in the CUOHROC.

119. William Adams Delano, "My Architectural Creed," *Pencil Points* 13 (March 1932): 145.

120. Delano's father, Eugene Delano (1843–1920), brother, Moreau Delano (1877–1936), uncle, John Crosby Brown (1838–1909) and first cousins, James Crosby Brown (1872–1930) and Thatcher Magoun Brown (1876–1954) were partners at Brown Brothers & Company. This factor must have contributed to Delano & Aldrich's involvement in the firm's building campaigns. In addition to designing two earlier additions to the firm's 1865 building of the same site, Delano & Aldrich also designed Brown Brothers' Philadelphia office in 1926. Articles on the building include "View of Brown Bros. & Co.'s Building, New York," *Architectural Record* 45 (June 1919): 559–60; "Private Office, Brown Bros. & Co., 59 Wall Street, New York," *The Architect* (Janu-

ary 1924): pl. 92; "Fifty Nine Wall Street, Brown Brothers & Co., December 1920," Delano & Aldrich Collection, Avery Architectural and Fine Arts Library, Columbia University in the City of New York; "63 Wall Street," Delano & Aldrich Collection, Avery Architectural and Fine Arts Library, Columbia University in the City of New York; "Architectural News in Photographs," *Architecture* 58 (August 1928): 87; "Architectural News in Photographs," *Architecture* 62 (August 1930): 80; "Office Building, Wall Street, New York," *Architecture and Building* 61 (June 1929): pls. 99–100; W. Parker Chase, "63 Wall Street Building," *New York: The Wonder City*, 1932 (New York: New York Bound, 1983), p. 159; Frank Scarlett, "An English Architect's Impressions of American Architecture and Allied Arts," *The American Architect* 135 (May 5, 1929): 561–68; John A. Kouwenhoven, *Partners in Banking: A Historical Portrait of a Great Private Bank* (New York: Doubleday, 1968).

121. Edward W. Wolner, "Design and Civic Identity in Cincinnati's Carew Tower Complex," *Journal of the Society of Architectural Historians* 51 (March 1992): 35–47. The Carew Tower is still the tallest building in Cincinnati.

122. "15–17 West 38th Street," *Architects' and Builders' Magazine* 41 (May 1909): 331–32; "The Architect: What He Has Done Recently and Why He Did It," *Real Estate Record and Guide* (1909): 337.

123. C. Matlack Price, "A Renaissance in Commercial Architecture," *Architectural Record* 31 (May 1912): 453–54.

124. "Apartments, 925 Park Avenue, New York," *Architecture* 19 (January 1909): 12, pl. 9; "925 Park Avenue, New York," *Architects' and Builders' Magazine* 41 (March 1909): 241–42.

125. "The New York Apartment of Condé Nast, Esq.," *Vogue* 72 (August 1, 1928): 44–47; Christopher Gray, "Streetscapes: 1040 Park Avenue," *The New York Times* (November 7, 1993), section 10, p. 8; "Apartment at 1040 Park Avenue, New York City," *Architectural Record* 67 (March 1930): 253; Caroline Seebohm, *The Man Who Was Vogue: The Life and Times of Condé Nast* (New York: Viking, 1982).

126. "Favorite Features," *Architecture* 70 (September 1934): 163; "American Red Cross Building, New York City," *Architecture and Building* 63 (May 1931).

127. The Society for the Preservation of Long Island Antiquities in Cold Spring Harbor, New York, has a Delano & Aldrich dollhouse is its collection.

128. William Adams Delano, "Memoirs of Centurian Architects: Part I," *Journal of the A.I.A.* 10 (July 1948): 8. The firm's competition entries included designs for: New Theater, New York City (1905), won by Carrère & Hastings; Waterbury City Hall, Waterbury, Connecticut (1913), won by Cass Gilbert; New York Court House (1912), won by Guy Lowell; Federal Reserve Bank, New York City (1919), won by York & Sawyer; Memorial to Theodore Roosevelt, Washington, D.C. (1925); Hartford County Building, Hartford, Connecticut (1927), won by Paul Cret; and Museum of the City of New York, New York City (1928), won by Joseph Freedlander.

129. In 1939, Delano & Aldrich was commissioned by Sir Kenneth Clark to design an addition to the National Gallery, which was to be financed by Calouste Sarkis Gulbenkian, a great art collector. Gulbenkian had selected Delano as architect based on the merit of his design for the American Government Building in Paris on the Place de la Concorde. In 1945, Delano & Aldrich won the competition for the Expansion Program at West Point; Shreve, Lamb & Harmon; Alfred Hopkins & Associates; and Skidmore, Owings & Merrill were runners-up. Delano & Aldrich completed a site plan for future development (1948) and modern Gothic additions to the Cadet Mess Hall and Gymnasium. However, plans for a new academic building, museum, nurses' quarters, and Cadet barracks were never realized; Congress refused to allocate money for the program.

130. In addition to their chapels integrated into a campus (Yale and Hotchkiss), Delano & Aldrich executed four free-standing churches: Clinton Farms Chapel, Clinton, New Jersey (1915); Third Church of Christ Scientist, New York City (1922–24); Dutch Reformed Church, Brookville, Long Island (1924); and First Church of Christ Scientist, Oyster Bay, Long Island (1931).

131. "Third Church of Christ Scientist," *Pencil Points* 6 (April 1925); "Third Church of Christ Scientist, Park Avenue, New York," *The American Architect—The Architectural Review* 125 (February 13, 1924); "Third Church of Christ Scientist is a Striking Edifice," *Real Estate Record and Guide* 113 (February 2, 1924): 9; "Third Church of Christ Scientist," *Architectural Forum* 40 (February 1924): pls. 18–21; "Third Church of Christ Scientist," *Architecture and Building* 56 (March 1924): pls. 57–58. After the completion of the Third Church of Christ Scientist, Delano continued to use Foster Gunnison to execute his designs for lighting fixtures. According to G. H. Edgell, the Christian Scientists wanted

to set themselves apart from older religious sects with definitive architecture.

132. "Third Church of Christ Scientist is a Striking Edifice," p. 9.

133. Howard Robertson, "Distinction in Architecture: The Work of Delano & Aldrich," *The Architect and Building News* 122 (November 29, 1929): 670; "Architecture's Portfolio of Spires," *Architecture* 70 (September 1934): 170. Delano contributed the design to the Dutch Reformed Church after its original house of worship burned.

134. "Sketches for Westminster Presbyterian Church, Albany, N. Y. as proposed by Delano & Aldrich, Architects," Westminster Presbyterian Church; "Crescent Avenue Presbyterian Parish House, Plainfield, New Jersey," *Architectural Record* 72 (October 1932): 241–43; "Christ Church Parish House, Hartford, Conn., Delano & Aldrich, Architects," *Architectural Record* 51 (April 1922): 315–16.

135. Delano's buildings at Yale included Wright Memorial Hall (1911–12), Sterling Chemistry Laboratory (1921–23), Sage Hall of Forestry (1922–24), William L. Harkness Hall (1925–26), Alpha Chi Rho Fraternity (1930), and Bowers Hall (1931).

136. "Willard Straight Hall, Cornell University, Ithaca, N.Y.," *Architecture and Building* 59 (March 1927): 72–3, 88–91; Herbert Croly, "Willard Straight Hall," *Architectural Record* 63 (June 1928): 545; "Mural Paintings by J. Monroe Hewlett in the Willard Straight Theatre," *American Magazine of Art* 17 (June 1926): 261; "Theatre, Willard Straight Hall, Cornell University," Architectural League of New York Yearbook, 1926; "Willard Straight Hall, Cornell University, Ithaca, New York," Architectural League of New York Yearbook, 1928.

137. "Sterling Chemistry Laboratory, Yale University," *Architecture* 48/47 (January/December 1923): 377–79; Harry S. Waterbury, "Designing and Planning Laboratory Buildings," *Architectural Forum* 44 (June 1926): 377–400.

138. William Adams Delano, "Memoirs of Centurian Architects: Part II," *Journal of the A.I.A.* 10 (August 1948): 84.

139. *The Reminiscences of William Adams Delano*, February 1950, page 54 in the CUOHROC.

140. "School of Music (Sage Hall), Smith College, Northampton, Massachusetts," *The American Architect* 129 (May 5, 1926): pls. 97–101; "Smith College Music Hall, Northampton, Mass.," Architectural League of New York Yearbook, 1926.

141. William Adams Delano to Ernest Rich, Lawrenceville, May 7, 1945. William Adams Delano Papers. Manuscripts and Archives, Yale University Library.

142. *The Reminiscences of William Adams Delano*, February 1950, page 54 in the CUOHROC.

143. Lewis Mumford, "The Skyline: The Architects Show Their Wares," *The New Yorker* 9 (March 4, 1933).

144. Patrick L. Pinnell, *The Campus Guide: Yale University* (New York: Princeton Architectural Press, 1999), pp. 160–62; "Yale Trains for the Ministry," *Yale Alumni Magazine* (October 1955); Paul Goldberger, "Architectural View: Saving a Beloved Chapel by Cutting out its Soul," *The New York Times*, section 2 (December 22, 1996), p. 49; "The Yale Divinity School, New Haven, Conn., Delano & Aldrich, Architects," *Architecture* 67 (May 1933): 269–74; Philip Langdon, "A Pattern of Destruction," *Preservation News* 49 (March/April 1997): 14–15; "Architectural News in Photographs," *Architecture* 62 (September 1930): 144; "Sterling Divinity Quadrangle, July 25, 1930," Manuscripts and Archives, Yale University Library. The campus was originally designed for a flat site on Hillhouse Avenue.

145. Witold Rybczynski, "Olmsted's Informal Landscapes Fit Far Better in a Chaotic Democracy than their Formalist Counterparts," *Architectural Record* 187 (November 1999): 29–30. Kinnan Gateway, marking the school's main entrance, is detailed with turtles and corn. A Lawrenceville student, writing an article for the school's newspaper, asked Delano to explain the significance of the motifs. Delano responded that they were "purely decorative motives to fill the space." William Adams Delano to Bruce Paton, student at Lawrenceville, February 3, 1955. William Adams Delano Papers. Manuscripts and Archives, Yale University Library. Unfortunately Delano's comment does not elucidate the reasoning behind the motif; his attachment to turtles, fish, dolphins, and other sea motifs is quite apparent in his work.

146. "Interior of New Chapel, Hotchkiss School, Lakeville, Conn.," Architectural League of New York Yearbook, 1932; Delano & Aldrich Collection, Avery Architectural and Fine Arts Library, Columbia University in the City of New York.

147. "The Philadelphia Orphanage at Wallingford, Pa.," *The New York Architect* 2 (June 1908). Delano's mother had been a member of the board of trustees of the Philadelphia Orphanage when the family lived in Philadelphia. The orphanage was not an orphanage per se; rather, it was home to children from broken families. As an early project, the young firm was still learning. According

to Delano, after the plans for the building were complete, they realized that the walls would not have carried the floor spans safely. The contractor, however, had also realized their miscalculations and had corrected their mistake before it became an issue.

148. As a board member of the International Grenfell Association, Delano donated designs for several hospitals and orphanages to the organization. Delano met Sir Wilfred Grenfell when Grenfell came to New York in the early 1900s with letters of introduction to Delano's father. A young doctor for the Royal National Mission to Deep Sea Fishermen, Grenfell was interested in raising funds to finance a medical mission to the bleak, uncharted coast of the Labradors and Newfoundland. His zeal and enthusiasm were contagious; both Delano and his father quickly became involved with the cause and the International Grenfell Association was born. Accounts of Delano's visit to Newfoundland in 1926 and adventures aboard Grenfell's hospital ship, *Strathcona*, can be found in *The Reminiscences of William Adams Delano* and William Adams Delano, "Of Men and Fish," *Among the Deep Sea Fishers* (April 1954): 18–19. Delano & Aldrich's Twillingate Hospital for Dr. C. E. Parsons (1923–24) and St. Clare's Mercy Hospital St. John's, Newfoundland for E. P. Roche (1938–39) were also stripped, rectilinear buildings with a hint of architectural definition surrounding the main entrance.

149. "Private Pavilion of the Flower Hospital, New York," *Architecture and Building* 46 (August 1914): 367.

150. Delano & Aldrich Collection, Avery Architectural and Fine Arts Library, Columbia University in the City of New York. Prentiss L Coonley, who lived in neighboring Great Barrington, was president of the Austen Riggs Foundation in 1939 and chairman of the board 1943–46. His house, a stone cottage-style mansion called Folly Farm (1930–31), was also designed by the firm and built concurrently.

151. "The Howard Gardner Cushing Art Gallery at Newport, Rhode Island, Delano & Aldrich, Architects," *Architectural Review* 12 (1921): 12–14, pl. 8. Original plans included in *Architectural Review* detailed a much larger scheme; the gallery was to be one wing of the proposed building for the Newport Art Association, all designed by Delano & Aldrich. The proposed building consisted of a central domed section with portico and symmetrical, arcaded hyphens on either side connected to two identical smaller pavilions, one of which was the Cushing Memorial Art Gallery. The central portion of the building was to house a hall of casts and rooms for special exhibitions, and the second pavilion would house a lecture hall. Gertrude Vanderbilt Whitney was also involved in the project, raising funds to finance the memorial.

152. "Staten Island Savings Bank, Stapleton, Staten Island," Architectural League of New York Yearbook, 1926; "Staten Island Savings Bank, Stapleton, S. I.," *Architecture and Building* 57 (February 1925): 14, 19; pls. 38–39.

153. Gilmore D. Clarke, "Collaboration in Bridge Design, I. The Architect," *Architectural Forum* 48 (May 1928): 729–34; Leslie G. Holleran, "Collaboration in Bridge Design, II. The Engineer," *The Architectural Forum* 48 (May 1928): 735–38; Arthur G. Hayden, "Two Parkway Bridges Planned by Engineer and Architect," *Engineering News-Record* 95 (July 2, 1925): 16–19. Firms such as Carrère & Hastings and Palmer & Hornbostel, and architects Gilmore D. Clarke and Charles W. Stoughton designed additional bridges for the commission.

154. "Lauxmont Dairy at Wrightsville, Pennsylvania, Delano and Aldrich, Architects," *Architectural Record* 76 (September 1934): 191–99.

155. The Board of Architectural Consultants consisted of Edward Bennett (chairman) of Bennett Parsons & Frost; Louis Ayres of York & Sawyer, New York, Arthur Brown, Jr., of San Francisco; Milton B. Medary of Zantzinger, Borie & Medary, Philadelphia, (succeeded on Medary's death by partner Clarence C. Zantzinger); John Russell Pope of New York; and William Adams Delano of Delano & Aldrich, New York.

156. Edwin Bateman Morris, "The City of Washington Today," *Architecture* 68 (October 1933): 189–204; "A Letter from Mr. William Adams Delano," *The Federal Architect* 12 (January–April 1943): 19; "The Editor's Asides," *Journal of the A.I.A.* 3 (January 1945): 44–45; William Adams Delano, "The Triangle Group," *Journal of the A.I.A.* 3 (March 1945): 121; William Harlan Hale, "The Grandeur that is Washington," *Harper's Monthly Magazine* 168 (April 1934): 560–69; John W. Reps, *Monumental Washington: the Planning and Development of the Capital Center* (Princeton, N.J.: Princeton University Press, 1967), pp. 169–77; Sue A. Kohler, *The Commission of Fine Arts: A Brief History, 1910–1976* (Washington: U.S. Government Printing Office, 1977), pp. 52–66; Sally Kress Tompkins, *A Quest for Grandeur: Charles Moore and the Federal Triangle* (Washington: Smithsonian

Institute Press, 1993); "Architectural News in Photographs," *Architecture* 71 (February 1935): 80; "Post Office Department Building, Washington, D.C.," *Architectural Forum* 55 (September 1931): 263; "Order and Scale in City Building with Reference to Public Buildings in Washington," *Landscape Architecture* 20 (April 1930): 188–91.

157. L'Enfant was a French engineer and artist who befriended George Washington while serving in the Revolutionary War. His formal vision of 1791 mapped a system of broad avenues and open spaces in which important sites and buildings—such as the houses of Congress and the President—were to be located in key spots and visually linked with one another. It consisted of a grid pattern with an overlay of wide, diagonal avenues—which now form the Federal Triangle—radiating out from significant sites. The Senate Park Commission plan of 1901, under Michigan senator James McMillan, developed L'Enfant's plan. A committee composed of Daniel Burnham, Charles McKim, Frederick Law Olmsted, Jr., and Augustus Saint-Gaudens prepared a plan to develop the city and locate new buildings. One feature of their plan included developing the triangular lot formed by Pennsylvania Avenue, 15th Street, and the Mall into a coordinated, governmental office complex. The National Commission of Fine Arts was established in 1910 under Taft to guide all of the design of the new development initiated by plan. Charles Moore, McMillan's secretary, became the chair of the commission.

158. Andrew Mellon as quoted in Henry Hope Reed, *The Golden City* (New York: Norton, 1959), p. 98.

159. William Adams Delano, "Foreword," in R. W. Sexton, ed., *American Public Building of To-Day* (New York: Architectural Book Publishing, 1931), p. i.

160. Reed, *The Golden City*, p. 96.

161. "The New U.S. Government Building in Paris," *Architecture* 70 (September 1934): 121–28; William Adams Delano, "Working for the Government," Delano & Aldrich Collection, Avery Architectural and Fine Arts Library, Columbia University in the City of New York; Jane C. Loeffler, *The Architecture of Diplomacy: Building America's Embassies* (New York: Princeton Architectural Press, 1998), pp. 29–31; "Architectural News in Photographs," *Architecture* 64 (September 1931): 148; "The American Government Building, Paris, November 1933," Delano & Aldrich Collection, Avery Architectural and Fine Arts Library, Columbia University in the City of New York; William Adams Delano,

"The American Government Building in Paris," publication unknown. Delano & Aldrich Collection, Avery Architectural and Fine Arts Library, Columbia University in the City of New York.

162. "Architectural News in Photographs," *Architecture* 62 (August 1930): 81; Delano & Aldrich Collection, Avery Architectural and Fine Arts Library, Columbia University in the City of New York.

163. Drawings for the Ellis Island ferry house were prepared by the Public Building Branch of the Procurement Division of the Treasury Department. Louis A. Simon acted as supervising architect and Chester Aldrich as consulting architect.

164. An extended discussion of the World's Fair can be found in Robert A. M. Stern, Gregory Gilmartin, and Thomas Mellins, *New York 1930: Architecture and Urbanism between the Two World Wars* (New York: Rizzoli, 1988), pp. 727–57.

165. As quoted by Harmon Goldstone in Victoria Newhouse, *Wallace K. Harrison, Architect* (New York: Rizzoli, 1989), p. 89.

166. "Epinal American Cemetery and Memorial," in Elizabeth Nishium, ed., *A Guide to Military Cemeteries and Monuments Maintained by the American Battle Monuments Commission* (Detroit, Mich.: Omnigraphics, 1989), pp. 173–88; William Adams Delano, "In Humble Tribute," *Think* 19 (April 1953): 12–13, 32.

167. Ron Robin, *Enclaves of America: The Rhetoric of American Political Architecture Abroad, 1900–1965* (Princeton, N.J.: Princeton University Press, 1992), pp. 109–35. Paul Cret has often been considered the master of stripped classical idiom. With such designs as the Folger Shakespeare Library (1929) and Federal Reserve Board Building in Washington, D.C. (1935), the Beaux-Arts–trained architect developed a modern monumental architecture that derived its power from undecorated surfaces, simplified classical motifs, and classical proportion. In setting Cret's example as a model for design, the American Battle Monuments Commission found a middle ground in the ongoing architectural debate between the traditional and modernist camps. Delano admired Paul Cret and identified with his work. In writing to Paul Cret's widow, Delano wrote of Cret, "We had fundamentally the same point of view about our work, a view which lay between tradition and extreme modernism." Delano to Mrs. Cret, September 12, 1945. William Adams Delano Papers. Manuscripts and Archives, Yale University Library. John Harbeson, who had been a partner in Cret's firm in

Philadelphia, supervised the design of the war memorials. All of the architects involved with the project were recommended by the National Commission of Fine Arts.

168. "The South Portico of the White House," *Journal of the A. I. A.* 9 (February 1948): 64–72.

169. While there is some question as to how the association between Pan American Airways and Delano & Aldrich came about, it is clear that the architects operated within the same circles as those interested in aviation and its expansion. Juan Trippe had graduated from Yale (1921); Delano had friends on the board of the Aviation Corporation who backed Pan American's venture; Aldrich's sister, Amey, and Charles Lindbergh's mother-in-law, Elizabeth Morrow, were best friends. This connection mostly likely led to several Delano & Aldrich commissions for the Morrow family, including houses in Englewood, New Jersey, and North Haven, Maine, dating from 1927. Delano & Aldrich also designed the Lindberghs' house in Hopewell, New Jersey, in 1931.

170. *The American Architect* 136 (July 20, 1929): 76.

171. David Brodherson, "An Airport in Every City: The History of American Airport Design," in John Zutowsky, ed., *Building for Air Travel: Architecture and Design for Commercial Aviation* (New York: Prestel-Verlag, 1996).

172. *The American Architect* 135 (April 5, 1929): 438; *The American Architect* 136 (July 20, 1929): 76–77; "Pan American Airways System: Miami Terminal to Incorporate Most Advanced Ideas in Airport Design and Operation," *Airway Age* 9 (November 1928): 34–37; Roger W. Sherman, "Planning for Airport Buildings," *Architectural Forum* 53 (December 1930): 731–32; Brodherson, "An Airport in Every City," pp. 69–70.

173. William Adams Delano, "Aviation's Growing Pains Reflected at Idlewild," *Herald Tribune* (October 10, 1948).

174. John Walter Wood, *Airports: Some Elements of Design and Future Development* (New York: Coward McCann, c. 1940), pp. 91–97; "The Miami Airport, International Air Terminal of the Pan American Airways System, Delano & Aldrich, Architects," *Architecture* 71 (April 1935): 195–202; "Gateway to the Americas," *Pan American Air Ways* 4 (June 1933); "Pan American's New Aerial Terminal at Miami Nears Completion," *Pan American Air Ways* 5 (March 1934); "Behind the Scenes at New International Airport," *Pan American Air Ways* 5 (September/October 1934): 23; Brodherson, "An Airport for Every City," p. 74.

175. Delano & Aldrich Collection, Avery Architectural and Fine Arts Library, Columbia University in the City of New York; Jack E. Robinson, *American Icarus: The Majestic Rise and Tragic fall of Pan Am* (Baltimore, Md.: Noble House, 1994), pp. 44–82. On November 22, 1935, the first transpacific flight departed from Alameda, California; almost 60 hours and 8,210 miles later, it arrived in Manila. Pearl Harbor and the onset of World War II brought the golden era of the Pacific and its Clippers to an abrupt end. Facilities at Midway, Wake, and Guam were either damaged or destroyed during the war, and technological advances in aviation soon rendered the Clipper ship obsolete.

176. *The Reminiscences of William Adams Delano*, February 1950, pages 9–10 in the CUOHROC. Delano & Aldrich also designed emergency bases in Charlestown and Baltimore. The Delano & Aldrich archives also contain drawings for a seaplane base in Brownsville, Texas, but it is unclear whether the terminal was ever constructed. Originally the airport was named New York Municipal Airport at North Beach. However, in 1939, the Board of Estimate and the City Council decided to rename the airport New York Municipal Airport, LaGuardia Field in honor of the mayor who conceived it.

177. New York Landmarks Preservation Commission, *Marine Air Terminal, LaGuardia Airport, Borough of Queens* (New York: Landmarks Preservation Commission, 1980); New York Landmarks Preservation Commission, *Marine Air Terminal Interior* (New York: Landmarks Preservation Commission, 1980); Christopher Gray, "Streetscapes: Marine Air Terminal: Restoring the Landmark Home of the Flying Fish," *The New York Times*, section 9 (October 1, 1995), p. 7; Geoffrey Arend, *LaGuardia: 1939–1979* (New York: Air Cargo News, 1979); Lewis Mumford, "Millions for Mausoleums," *The New Yorker* 15 (December 30, 1939): 49–50; "New York Airport," *The Architects' Journal* 93 (March 20, 1941): 195–99; Stern et al., *New York 1930*, pp. 702–4; "New York Municipal Airport," Work Projects Administration. William Adams Delano Papers. Manuscripts and Archives, Yale University Library; Wood, *Airports*, pp. 113–18; Major A. B. McMullen, "The Development of Airports," *Pencil Points* 21 (October 1940): 613–32; *Pencil Points* 19 (January 1938): 2, 19; "Program of Events: New York Municipal Airport Dedication, North Beach, Long Island, Sunday, October Fifteenth, 1939," Delano & Aldrich Collection. Avery

Architectural and Fine Arts Library, Columbia University in the City of New York; "North Beach Airport: New York's Municipal Airport," *Engineering News-Record* 124 (March 28, 1940): 61–72; David Brodherson, "An Airport for Every City," pp. 67–95; Robert A. M. Stern, Thomas Mellins, and David Fishman, *New York 1960: Architecture and Urbanism between the Second World War and the Bicentennial* (New York: Monacelli Press, 1995), pp. 989–92.

178. "New York's Airport for World Commerce," *Engineering News-Record* 136 (January 24, 1946): 76.

179. Delano's centralized terminal did not take into account the airlines' individual identities or the potential for competition between companies; it was Delano's intention that the administration building be the focal point of the design in which all the airways—big or small—be put on equal footing. With the discovery that twelve tangential runways moved air traffic faster, Delano's design, based on a dual parallel system, became outmoded. To accommodate the increased number of passengers, the airlines wanted 100 gates, spaced at 150-foot intervals, which would have resulted in an ungainly three-mile loading platform. Among his innovations, Delano proposed to Port Authority the idea of the "ladder bus," a vehicle with an adjustable floor level that would carry passengers from the gates to the planes. "Finest Airport in the Word," *The New York Times Magazine*, section 6 (January 21, 1945), pp. 10–11, 43; "Airport Architecture," *The New York Times*, section 6 (February 25, 1945), p. 12. "Municipal Airport at Idlewild," Department of Marine and Aviation, City of New York, April 1945; "Aviation's Growing Pains Reflected at Idlewild," *Herald Tribune* (October 10, 1948); Brodherson, "An Airport in Every City," p. 86; Stern et al., *New York 1960*, pp. 1006–8.

180. "The Gold Medal of Honor," *Journal of the A.I.A.* 19 (June 1953): 262–63.

181. Richard Guy Wilson, *The A.I.A. Gold Medal* (New York: McGraw Hill, 1984), pp. 61–83.

TWENTY DELANO & ALDRICH PROJECTS

1. *The Reminiscences of William Adams Delano*, February 1950, pages 9–10 in the CUOHROC.

2. Johnston, *William and Henry Walters*, p. 168.

3. Brendan Gill, "William Adams Delano—Gentleman Architect," *Architectural Digest* 47 (December 1990): 88, 90, 94, 96; Brendan Gill, *A New York Life: Of Friends and Others* (New York: Poseidon Press, 1990), p. 92.

4. Carole Owens, *The Berkshire Cottages: A Vanishing Era* (Stockbridge, Mass.: Cottage Press, 1984), p. 20.

5. *The Reminiscences of William Adams Delano*, February 1950, page 13 in the CUOHROC.

6. *The Reminiscences of William Adams Delano*, February 1950, page 27 in the CUOHROC.

7. As quoted by Arthur Lee in Linda Nochlin, "High Bohemia," *House & Garden* 157 (September 1985): 234.

8. *The Reminiscences of William Adams Delano*, February 1950, pages 13–14 in the CUOHROC.

9. Cleveland Amory, *Who Killed Society?* (New York: Harper & Brothers, 1960), p. 203; William J. Dunn, *Knickerbocker Centennial: An Informal History of the Knickerbocker Club, 1871–1971* (New York: Knickerbocker Club, 1971).

10. *The Reminiscences of William Adams Delano*, February 1950, page 11 in the CUOHROC.

11. "Painted Fish on a Painted Sea," in Richardson Wright and M. McElroy, eds., *House and Garden's Book on Color Schemes* (New York: Condé Nast Publications, c. 1929), pp. 163–64.

12. *The Reminiscences of William Adams Delano*, February 1950, pages 28–29 in the CUOHROC.

13. Cortissoz, *Portraits of Ten Country Houses*, p. xiv.

14. Drexler, *The Architecture of the Ecole des Beaux-Arts*, p. 489.

15. Dorothy Nichols, "A Great American Garden," *Country Life* 79 (April 1941): 26.

16. *The Reminiscences of William Adams Delano*, February 1950, page 19 in the CUOHROC.

17. *The Reminiscences of William Adams Delano*, February 1950, pages 29–30 in the CUOHROC.

18. Cortissoz, *Portraits of Ten Country Houses*, p. xii.

19. *The Reminiscences of William Adams Delano*, February 1950, page 21 in the CUOHROC.

20. Harriet Pratt, Letter to William Adams Delano, January 3, 1946; William Adams Delano, Letter to Mr. Fisher, June 12, 1951. Delano's name also appears on the cornerstone of the U.S. Government Building in Paris.

21. *The Reminiscences of William Adams Delano*, February 1950, page 43 in the CUOHROC.

22. *The Reminiscences of William Adams Delano*, February 1950, page 15 in the CUOHROC.

23. Murchison, "Mr. Murchison of New York Says—," p. 351.

24. Townsend, *Mother of Clubs*, p. 103.
25. Delano wrote this limerick in the Emerys' guest book at Peterloon, December 1937.
26. Edward W. Wolner, "Design and Civic Identity in Cincinnati's Carew Tower Complex," *Journal of the Society of Architectural Historians* 51 (March 1992): 35–47; "Architectural News in Photographs," *Architecture* 63 (January 1931): 21; "Carew Tower, Cincinnati, Ohio," *Architecture and Building* 63 (February 1931): 34.
27. *The Reminiscences of William Adams Delano*, February 1950, page 62 in the CUOHROC.
28. Letter from Miss Manning, Delano's secretary, to Mr. Myron Hendee, U.S. Department of Agriculture Graduate School, June 3, 1958. William Adams Delano Papers. Manuscripts and Archives, Yale University Library. According to Sally Kress Tompkins, *A Quest for Grandeur*, the building's fourth floor lobby contains murals by Reginald Marsh and the anteroom of postmaster general's reception room contains six aluminum statues of postmen in niches, including Chaim Gross's *Alaska Snowshoe Mail Carrier* and Louis Slobodkin's *Hawaiian Postman*.
29. William Harlan Hale, "The Grandeur that is Washington," *Harper's Monthly Magazine* 168 (April 1934): 560–69.
30. Delano, "Foreword," p. i.
31. William Adams Delano, "Order and Scale in City Building with Reference to Public Buildings in Washington," *Landscape Architecture* 20 (April 1930): 188.
32. *The Reminiscences of William Adams Delano*, February 1950, pages 83–84 in the CUOHROC.
33. Brodherson, "An Airport in Every City," p. 77.
34. Wood, *Airports*, p. 118.

BIBLIOGRAPHY

"Architects in Washington." *Time* 15 (June 2, 1930): 24–28.

Aslet, Clive. *The American Country House.* New Haven, Conn.: Yale University Press, 1990.

Axelrod, Alan, ed. *The Colonial Revival in America.* New York: W. W. Norton & Company, 1985.

Bedford, Steven. *John Russell Pope, Architect of Empire.* New York: Rizzoli International Publications, 1998.

Bottomley, William Lawrence. "A Selection from the Works of Delano & Aldrich, Drawings by Chester B. Price." *Architectural Record* 54 (July 1923): 2–71.

Brown, Elizabeth. *New Haven: A Guide to Architecture and Urban Design.* New Haven, Conn.: Yale University Press, 1976.

Burchard, John, and Albert Bush–Brown. *The Architecture of America: A Social and Cultural History.* Boston: Little Brown and Company, 1961.

Burnham, Alan. *New York Landmarks.* Middletown, Conn.: Wesleyan University Press, 1963.

Cable, Mary. *Top Drawer: American High Society from the Gilded Age to the Roaring Twenties.* New York: Atheneum, 1984.

Capitman, Barbara Baer. *Rediscovering Art Deco U.S.A.* New York: Viking Studio Books, 1994.

Cleveland, Amory. *Who Killed Society?* New York: Harper & Brothers, 1960.

De Penanrun, David, Roux and Delaire. *Les Architectes: Élèves de L'École des Beaux-Arts.* Paris: Librarie de la Construction Moderne, 1907.

Delano, William A., and Chester Aldrich. *Portraits of Ten Country Houses.* Introduction by Royal Cortissoz. Garden City, N.Y.: Doubleday, Page & Company, 1924.

Diamondstein, Barbaralee. *The Landmarks of New York.* New York: Harry N. Abrams, 1988.

Dolkart, Andrew S. *Touring the Upper East Side: Walks in the Five Historic Districts.* New York: New York Landmarks Conservancy, 1995.

Drexler, Arthur. *The Architecture of the Ecole des Beaux-Arts.* Cambridge, Mass.: MIT Press, 1977.

Edgell, George Harold. *American Architecture of To–Day.* New York: Scribner's, 1928.

Elwood, P. H., Jr., ed. *American Landscape Architecture.* New York: Architectural Book Publishing, 1924.

Embury, Aymar, II. *One Hundred Country Houses.* New York: The Century Company, 1909.

———. *The Livable House: Its Plan and Design.* New York: Moffat Yard & Company, 1917.

———, ed. *The Livable House: Its Gardens, Volume Two.* New York: Moffat Yard & Company, 1917.

Fahlman, Betsy, "Delano and Aldrich," in *A Biographical Dictionary of Architects in Maine.* Augusta, Maine: Maine Historic Preservation Commission, 1995.

Folsom, Merrill. *Great American Mansions & Their Stories.* New York: Hastings House Publishers, 1963.

Gebhard, David. *The National Trust Guide to Art Deco in America.* New York: John Wiley & Sons, c. 1996.

Gill, Brendan. "William Adams Delano— Gentleman Architect." *Architectural Digest* 47 (December 1990): 88, 90, 94, 96.

Griswold, Mac, and Eleanor Weller. *The Golden Age of American Gardens, Proud Owners, Private Estates, 1890–1940.* New York: Harry N. Abrams, 1991.

Grossman, Elizabeth Greenwell. *The Civic Architecture of Paul Cret.* New York: Cambridge University Press, 1996.

Hamlin, Talbot Faulkner. *The Pageant of America: The American Spirit in Architecture.* New Haven, Conn.: Yale University Press, 1926.

Hering, Oswald C. *Building Concrete & Stucco Houses.* New York: Robert M. McBride & Company, 1929.

Hewitt, Mark. *The Architect and the American Country House 1890–1940.* New Haven, Conn.: Yale University Press, 1990.

———. *The Architecture of Mott B. Schmidt.* New York: Rizzoli International Publications, 1991.

Howe, Samuel. *American Country Houses of To–day.* New York: Architectural Book Publishing Company, 1915.

Howell, E. W. *Noted Long Island Homes.* Babylon, N.Y.: E. W. Howell, 1933.

Keefe, Charles S., ed. *The American House: Being a Collection of Illustrations and Plans of the Best Country and Suburban Houses Built in the United States during the Last Few Years.* New York: U.P.C. Book Company, 1922.

Kidney, Walter C. *The Architecture of Choice: Eclecticism in America 1880–1930.* New York: George Braziller, 1974.

Kimball, Fiske. "The American Country House." *Architectural Record* 46 (October 1919): 297–400.

Kocher, A. Lawrence. "The Country House: An Analysis of the Architect's Method of Approach." *Architectural Record* 62 (November 1927): 337–448.

Lindeberg, H. T. *Domestic Architecture of H. T. Lindeberg.* New York: Acanthus Press, 1996.

Longstreth, Richard W. "Academic Eclecticism in American Architecture." *Winterthur Portfolio* 17 (Spring 1982): 55–82.

"Luxurious American Country Houses," *Arts & Decoration* 23 (July 1925): pp. 42–44.

The Long Island Country House: 1870–1930. Southampton, New York: Parrish Art Museum, 1988.

MacKay, Robert B., Anthony K. Baker, and Carol A. Traynor. *Long Island Country Houses and Their Architects, 1860–1940.* New York: W. W. Norton & Company, 1997.

Mitchell, William R., Jr. *Landmarks: The Architecture of Thomasville and Thomas County, Georgia: 1820–1980.* Thomasville, Ga.: Thomasville Landmarks, 1980.

Morgan Keith N. *Shaping an American Landscape: The Art and Architecture of Charles A. Platt.* Hanover, N.H.: University Press of New England, 1995.

———. *Charles A. Platt, the Artist as Architect.* Cambridge, Mass.: MIT Press, 1985.

Nevins, Deborah. *Between Traditions and Modernism: American Architectural Drawings from the National Academy of Design.* New York: National Academy of Design, 1980.

Newhouse, Victoria. *Wallace K. Harrison, Architect.* New York: Rizzoli International Publications, 1989.

Noffsinger, James Philip. *The Influence of the Ecole des Beaux-Arts on the Architects of the United States.* Washington: Catholic University of America Press, 1955.

Oliver, Richard, ed. *The Making of an Architect, 1881–1981: Columbia University in the City of New York.* New York: Rizzoli International Publications, 1981.

Owens, Carole. *The Berkshire Cottages: A Vanishing Era.* Englewood Cliffs, N.J.: Cottage Press, 1984.

Patterson, Augusta Owen. *American Homes of To–day: Their Architectural Style, Their Environment, Their Characteristics.* New York: Macmillan, 1924.

Randall, Monica. *Mansions of Long Island's Gold Coast.* New York: Rizzoli International Publications, 1987.

Reed, Henry Hope. *The Golden City.* New York: W. W. Norton & Company, 1959.

Rhoads, William B. *The Colonial Revival.* New York and London: Garland Publishing, 1977.

Robertson, Howard. "Distinction in Architecture: The Work of the New York Architects, Delano & Aldrich." *The Architect & Building News* 122 (November 22 and 29, 1929): 629–34, 670–74.

Salny, Stephen M. *The Country Houses of David Adler.* New York: W. W. Norton & Company, 2001.

Saylor, Henry H. ed. *Architectural Styles for Country Houses: the Characteristics and Merits of Various Types of Architecture as Set Forth by Enthusiastic Advocates.* New York: McBride, Nast, 1912.

Schnadelbach, R. Terry. Ferruccio *Vitale: Landscape Architect of the Country Place Era.* New York: Princeton Architectural Press, 2001.

Sclare, Lisa, and Donald Sclare. *Beaux–Arts Estates: A Guide to the Architecture of Long Island.* New York: Viking Press, 1979.

Sexton, R. W. *Interior Architecture.* New York: Architectural Book Publishing Company, 1927.

———, ed. *American Public Buildings of Today.* New York: Architectural Book Publishing Company, 1931.

Stern, Robert A. M. *George Howe: Toward a Modern American Architecture.* New Haven, Conn.: Yale University Press, 1975.

———, John Montague Massengale, and Gregory Gilmartin. *New York 1900: Metropolitan Architecture and Urbanism, 1890–1915.* New York: Rizzoli International Publications, 1983.

———, Gregory Gilmartin, and Thomas Mellins. *New York 1930: Architecture and Urbanism between the Two World Wars.* New York: Rizzoli International Publications, 1988.

———, Thomas Mellins, and David Fishman. *New York 1960: Architecture and Urbanism between the Second World War and the Bicentennial.* New York: Monacelli Press, 1995.

———. *New York 1880: Architecture and Urbanism in the Gilded Age.* New York: Monacelli Press, 1999.

Tallmadge, Thomas E. *The Story of Architecture in America.* New York: W. W. Norton & Company, 1936.

"The Talk of the Town: Architect." *The New Yorker* 34 (April 5, 1958): 23–24.

Tauranac, John. *Elegant New York: The Builders and the Buildings, 1885–1915.* New York: Abbeville Press, 1985.

Tompkins, Sally Kress. *A Quest for Grandeur: Charles Moore and the Federal Triangle.*

Washington: Smithsonian Institute Press, 1993.

Valentine, Lucia, and Alan Valentine. *The American Academy in Rome: 1849–1969.* Charlottesville: University Press of Virginia, 1973.

White, Samuel G. *The Houses of McKim, Mead & White.* New York: Rizzoli International Publications, 1998.

Wilson, Richard Guy. *The A.I. A. Gold Medal.* New York, McGraw–Hill, 1984.

———, and Dianne H. Pilgrim, eds. *The American Renaissance 1876–1917.* New York: Pantheon Books in association with the Brooklyn Museum, 1979.

Wright, Richardson, and M. McElroy, eds. *House and Garden's Book of Interiors.* New York: Condé Nast and Company, 1920.

———. *House and Garden's Second Book of Interiors.* New York: Condé Nast Publications, c. 1926.

———. *House and Garden's Book of Color Schemes.* New York: Condé Nast Publications, c. 1929.

UNPUBLISHED SOURCES

Centre Historique des Archives Nationales, Archives, École Nationale Superieure des Beaux-Arts, Paris, France.

Century Association Archives Foundation, 7 West 43rd Street, New York City.

Chester and Amey Aldrich scrapbooks at Rokeby, Barrytown, New York.

Delano & Aldrich Collection, Avery Architectural and Fine Arts Library, Columbia University in the City of New York.

Delano & Aldrich Collection, New–York Historical Society, New York City.

Delano, William Adams. *A Letter to my Grandson.* Delano & Aldrich Collection, Avery Architectural and Fine Arts Library, Columbia University in the City of New York.

Delano, William Adams. *Random Rhymes.* Manuscripts and Archives, Yale University, New Haven, Connecticut.

Gray, Erin Drake. *The Decorative Finishes Employed by Delano and Aldrich in the Principal Rooms of their Manhattan Clubs: The Knickerbocker, Colony and Union Clubs and the Brook.* New York: Columbia University, 1983.

Nevins, Alan, *The Reminiscences of William Adams Delano,* February 1950, in the Columbia University Oral History Research Office Collection.

Spinzia, Raymond E., and Judith A. Spinzia. *Long Island's Prominent North Shore Families: Their Estates and their Country Houses.* 1997 at the Nassau County Museum, Long Island Studies Institute, Hempstead, Long Island.

William Adams Delano Papers, Manuscripts and Archives, Yale University, New Haven, Connecticut.

ARTICLES BY WILLIAM ADAMS DELANO
AND CHESTER HOLMES ALDRICH

Aldrich, Chester. "How to Choose an Architect." *Liturgical Arts* (date unknown) from the Chester and Amey Aldrich scrapbooks at Rokeby, Barrytown, New York.

Delano, William Adams. "Artist and Artisan." *Journal of the A.I.A.* 9 (August 1921): 260–63.

Aldrich, Chester. "What is Modern Architecture?" *Architecture* 59 (January 1929): 1–4.

Delano, William Adams. "Order and Scale in City Building with Reference to Public Buildings in Washington." *Landscape Architecture* 20 (April 1930): 188.

Delano, William Adams. "To Be an Ideal Architect." *Pencil Points* 13 (February 1932): 105–6.

Delano, William Adams. "My Architectural Creed." *Pencil Points* 13 (March 1932): 145.

Aldrich, Chester. "Modernism and Publicity." *Shelter* 2 (April 1932): 24–26.

Delano, William Adams, "Man versus Mass," *Shelter* 2 (May 1932).

Delano, William Adams. "Further Thoughts on Contemporary Architecture." *Pencil Points* 13 (July 1932): 467–68.

Delano, William Adams. "My Daxian." *Pencil Points* 13 (November 1932): 735.

Delano, William Adams. "Hommage à Laloux." *Pencil Points* 18 (October 1937): 621.

Delano, William Adams. "Architecture is an Art." *Architectural Forum* 72 (April 1940): 16–18.

Delano, William Adams. "The Architect: Forgotten Man?" *The New York Times Magazine* 7 (April 21, 1940): 9, 14.

Delano, William Adams. "A Marriage of Convenience." *Journal of the A.I.A.* 1 (May 1944): 211–15.

Delano, William Adams. "The Triangle Group." *Journal of the A.I.A.* 3 (March 1945): 121.

Delano, William Adams. "Paul Phillippe Cret." *Journal of the A.I.A.* 4 (October 1945): 178.

Delano, William Adams. "Memoirs of Centurian Architects." *Journal of the A.I.A.* 10 (July–October 1948): 3–9, 81–87, 130–36, 180–84.

Delano, William Adams. "Standards of Behavior." *Journal of the A.I.A.* 11 (April 1949): 186.

Delano, William Adams. "In Humble Tribute." *Think* 19 (April 1953): 12–13, 32.

Delano, William Adams. "High Spots of Career." *Architectural Record* (May 1953): 9–11.

Delano, William Adams. "Accepting the Gold Medal." *Journal of the A.I.A.* 20 (August 1953): 55–56.

Delano, William Adams. "Of Men and Fish." *Among the Deep Sea Fishers* (April 1954): 18–19.

Delano, William Adams. "Miss M," *Journal of the A.I.A.* 26 (November 1956): 220.

ACKNOWLEDGMENTS

This book was first inspired by our work at the Knickerbocker and Colony Clubs where the architects' original drawings were found in the buildings they describe. Subsequently, both institutions generously donated these archives to the Delano & Aldrich Collection at Avery Architectural and Fine Arts Library at Columbia University. Mark Alan Hewitt and Richard Guy Wilson's scholarship on Delano & Aldrich, a starting point for our research, also inspired us.

For sharing their recollections of William Adams Delano and Chester Holmes Aldrich, we are most grateful to David Aldrich, J. Winthrop Aldrich, Louis S. Auchincloss, Minor Bishop, Barbara Farnell, Kay Leach, Frances Murer, Mrs. George Post, Henry Hope Reed, Walter Rothschild and Lela Steele. Among the many people and organizations who shared information or supported our work, we would like to thank: at the American Institute of Architects, Sarah Turner; at the Architectural League of New York, Teresa Harris; Brooke Astor; Louis Bofferding; at the Centre Historique des Archives Nationales, Claire Bechu; Kate Buford; Gilbert Butler; at the Century Association Archives Foundation, Russell Flinchum; at the Chapin School, Eleanor Southworth; at the Cushing Memorial Art Gallery, Nancy Grinnell; Richard Dickenson, Richmond County Borough Historian, Staten Island; at Friends of the Upper East Side Historic Districts, Anne Millard; Christopher Gray; Ashton Hawkins; at The Hotchkiss School, John Tuke and Nighat Saleemi; Alexandra and Philip Howard; at The Lawrenceville School, Jacqueline Haun; Kenneth F. Jackson; Richard Jenrette; Hugh McCauley; McKown family; Aleks Matviak; at the New York State Historical Association, Shelley Stocking; at the Nightingale-Bamford School, Robin Rooks; Helen Pennoyer; Jane Delano Ridder, Katie Ridder; at the Rockefeller Archive Center, Robert Battaly; at the Round Hill Club, Dennis Meermans; at the St. Bernard's School, Virginia Tracy; Thomas Gordon Smith; Ross Stevens; Bronson Trevor; Jack Turpin; Susan Wadsworth; Norman S. Walker, Jr.; James T. Wollen; and James Yarnall. The information contributed by all of the local historical societies, libraries, current house owners, and descendants of the original owners we contacted was integral to the compilation of the catalogue raisonné.

We are indebted to the following people and organizations for giving us access to the firm's buildings: at the American Embassy in Paris, Ambassador and Mrs. Howard H. Leach, David Buss, and Carl Edwards; Mr. and Mrs. Jacques Berghmans; Lila Berle; Robert Bienstock; at Brown Brothers Harriman, Hampton S. Lynch, Jr.; Paul Burghardt, III; at the Chelsea Center at the Muttontown Preserve, Brenda Spezio; at the Council on Foreign Relations, April Palmerlee; Alice Field; the Italian Cultural Institute; R. M. Kliment; at the Knickerbocker Club, William Bremenour and Christian Dewailly; Pamela LeBoutillier; Mrs. Paul Mellon; Kelly Melius; at the North Shore Unitarian Universalist Society, Kathy Zullo; Mr. and Mrs. Anthony Rivara; at the Russian Orthodox Church Outside of Russia, Rev. Andrei Sommer; at the Saint David's School, Donald Maiocco; Edward Smits; at the Town Club, Bruno Levy; at the Union Club, Charles Dorn; at the Walters Art Gallery, Jennifer Renard and Catherine Pierre; Peter Wilde; Stanley Woodward; and Lloyd Zuckerberg. The company of Gregory Gilmartin, William Irvine, Thomas Jayne, and Valerie Westcott made our visits especially productive.

We must also thank Angela Giral, Director, Janet Parks, Curator of Drawings and Archives, and Louis Di Gennaro at Columbia University's Avery Architectural and Fine Arts Library for their patient assistance. The staff of the Manuscript and Archives Division of the Yale University Library, where the William Adams Delano Papers are housed, and Huyler C. Held, Robert MacKay, and the Society for the Preservation of Long Island Antiquities were also extremely helpful. Mildred DeRiggi of the Long Island Studies Institute, Columbia University's Oral History Research Office, and the staff at the New York Historical Society and the Museum of the City of New York were particularly accommodating.

We are especially grateful to Robert A. M. Stern for his guidance and encouragement from the onset of this project; James Taylor for reading our manuscript and helping us organize and edit it; Stephanie Williams for her dedicated research assistance; and Jonathan Wallen for adding an extra dimension to this book with his exquisite photography. And finally, we must thank our editor, Nancy Green, at W. W. Norton & Company and our designer, Abigail Sturges.

MUSEUM LIST

The following are Delano & Aldrich buildings that are open
to the public as museums, memorials, and houses.

BELAIR MANSION
12207 Tulip Grove Drive
Bowie, Maryland 20715
(301) 809–3089
museumevents@cityofbowie.org
www.cityofbowie.org/comserv/museums.htm

CAMP SANTANONI
Santanoni Preserve
Route 28 North
Newcomb, New York 12852
(518) 834–9328
info@aarch.org
www.aarch.org

CUSHING MEMORIAL GALLERY
Newport Art Museum
76 Bellevue Avenue
Newport, Rhode Island 02840
(401) 848–8200
info@newportartmuseum.com
www.newportartmuseum.com

EPINAL AMERICAN CEMETERY AND MEMORIAL
American Battle Monuments Commission
Epinal, Vosges, France
US contact: (703) 696–6897
http://www.abmc.gov/ep.htm

GREY TOWERS
151 Grey Towers Drive
Milford, Pennsylvania 18337
(570) 296–9630
gtowers@pinchot.org
www.pinchot.org/gt

INTERNATIONAL GARDEN CLUB
Bartow–Pell Mansion
895 Shore Road
Pelham Bay Park
Bronx, New York 10464
(718) 885–1461
bartowpell@aol.com
www.bartowpellmansionmuseum.org

KYKUIT
Phillipsburg Manor–Visitor's Center, Route 9
Sleepy Hollow, New York 10591
(914) 631–9491
www.hudsonvalley.org

MERESTEAD
455 Byram Lake Road
Mount Kisco, New York 10549
(914) 666–4258
Open for visiting hours by appointment

PETERLOON FOUNDATION
8605 Hopewell Road
Indian Hill, Ohio 45242
(513) 791–7600
Open to groups and organizations
    by appointment

UNITED STATES PAVILION
AT THE VENICE BIENNALE
Solomon R. Guggenheim Foundation
Castello Gardens
Venice, Italy
Phone: +39.041.2405.411
info@guggenheim–venice.it
http://www.guggenheim.org
Open during the Venice Biennale—
    art and architecture exhibitions

WALTERS ART MUSEUM
600 North Charles Street
Baltimore, Maryland 21201
(410) 547–9000
info@thewalters.org
www.thewalters.org

WELWYN PRESERVE
Holocaust Memorial & Educational Center
    of Nassau County
100 Crescent Beach Road
Glen Cove, New York 11542
(516) 571–8040
www.holocaust–nassau.org

APPENDIX

EMPLOYEES OF DELANO & ALDRICH

According to Delano, approximately three hundred employees passed through the office during its fifty-year history. Known office records do not exist.

ASSOCIATES
Herbert Godwin (unknown–1945)
George A. Licht (1908–50)
James Stewardson (1906–1945)
Henry S. Waterbury (1904–53)
George T. Licht
Alexander McIlvaine
John W. Waterbury

ADDITIONAL KNOWN EMPLOYEES
David Aldrich
George Boggs Allison
Albert L. Best
Minor Bishop
Cyrus Bissell
André Lucien Blouin
F. Burnham Chapman
William Richard Potter Delano
Alexander Tilloch Galt Durnford
Carl F. Grieshaber
Bancel LaFarge
Francis Wilshire Roudebush
Harry W. Seckel
Harold Sterner
Ides van der Gracht
William Wurster

Josephine Manning (Delano's assistant, 1916–60)

INDEX

Numbers in italic refer to illustrations.
Numbers in boldface and preceded by "c" refer to color plates.